# Improving Learning through the Lifecourse

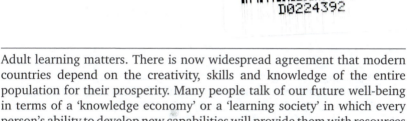

Adult learning matters. There is now widespread agreement that modern countries depend on the creativity, skills and knowledge of the entire population for their prosperity. Many people talk of our future well-being in terms of a 'knowledge economy' or a 'learning society' in which every person's ability to develop new capabilities will provide them with resources that will help them and the wider community to adapt and thrive. While in theory this makes lifelong learning into an exciting prospect, in practice this broad agenda is often reduced to a narrowly economic conception.

This book reports on one of the largest research projects into lifelong learning conducted in recent years. Through over 500 in-depth interviews with a cohort of about 120 adults who were followed for three years, the Learning Lives project has built up a detailed understanding of what learning means and does in the lives of adults. The project has generated insights in how learning has changed over time and across generations, what the connections are with the changing world of work, what differences learning makes for life chances, how we can learn from life and for life, and how people's prospects of learning can be improved. Combining life history and lifecourse research with analysis of longitudinal survey data, this book provides important insights into the learning biographies and trajectories of adults.

The book shows that learning means and does much more in people's lives than is often acknowledged by current education policy and politics. In doing so, it is an invaluable resource for anyone with an interest in the role and potential of learning through the lifecourse.

**Gert J. J. Biesta** is Professor of Education, University of Stirling, UK.

**John Field** is Professor of Lifelong Learning, University of Stirling, UK.

**Phil Hodkinson** is Emeritus Professor of Lifelong Learning, University of Leeds, UK.

**Flora J. Macleod** is a Senior Lecturer in Education, University of Exeter, UK.

**Ivor F. Goodson** is Professor of Learning Theory, University of Brighton, UK.

# Improving Learning TLRP

Series Editor: Andrew Pollard, Director of the ESRC Teaching and Learning Programme

The Improving Learning series showcases findings from projects within UK Economic and Social Research Council's (ESRC's) Teaching and Learning Research Programme (TLRP) – the UK's largest ever coordinated educational research initiative. Each book is explicitly designed to support 'evidence-informed' decisions in educational practice and policy making. In particular, they combine rigorous social and educational science with high awareness of the significance of the issues being researched.

**Improving Research through User Engagement**
*Mark Rickinson, Judy Sebba and Anne Edwards*

**Improving Literacy at Work**
*Alison Wolf and Karen Evans*

**Improving Mathematics at Work**
*Edited by Celia Hoyles, Richard Noss, Phillip Kent and Arthur Bakker*

**Improving the Context for Inclusion**
*Andy Howes, S.M.B. Davies and Sam Fox*

**Improving Working as Learning**
*Alan Felstead, Alison Fuller, Nick Jewson and Lorna Unwin*

**Improving Literacy by Teaching Morphemes**
*Terezinha Nunes and Peter Bryant*

**Improving Workplace Learning**
*Karen Evans, Phil Hodkinson, Helen Rainbird and Lorna Unwin*

**Improving Schools, Developing Inclusion**
*Mel Ainscow, Tony Booth and Alan Dyson*

**Improving Subject Teaching**
*Robin Millar, John Leach, Jonathan Osborne and Mary Ratcliffe*

**Improving Learning Cultures in Further Education**
David James and Gert J. J. Biesta

**Improving Learning How to Learn**
Mary James, Robert McCormick, Paul Black , Patrick Carmichael,
Mary-Jane Drummond, Alison Fox, John MacBeath, Bethan Marshall,
David Pedder, Richard Procter, Sue Swaffield, Joanna Swann
and Dylan Wiliam

**Improving Learning through Consulting Pupils**
Jean Rudduck and Donald McIntyre

**Improving Learning, Skills and Inclusion**
Frank Coffield, Sheila Edward, Ian Finlay, Ann Hodgson, Ken Spours and
Richard Steer

**Improving Classroom Learning with ICT**
Rosamund Sutherland

**Improving Learning in College**
Roz Ivanic, Richard Edwards, David Barton, Marilyn Martin-Jones,
Zoe Fowler, Buddug Hughes, Greg Mannion, Kate Miller, Candice Satchwell
and June Smith

**Improving Learning in Later Life**
Alexandra Withnall

**Improving Learning by Widening Participation in Higher
Education**
Edited by Miriam David

**Improving Research Through User Engagement**
Mark Rickinson, Anne Edwards and Judy Sebba

**Improving What is Learned at University**
John Brennan

**Improving Inter-professional Collaborations**
Anne Edwards, Harry Daniels, Tony Gallagher, Jane Leadbetter and
Paul Warmington

**Improving Learning in a Professional Context**
Edited by Jim McNally and Allan Blake

**Improving Disabled Students' Learning**
Mary Fuller, Jan Georgeson, Mick Healey, Alan Hurst, Katie Kelly, Sheila
Riddell, Hazel Roberts and Elizabet Weedon

# Improving Learning through the Lifecourse

## Learning Lives

Gert J. J. Biesta, John Field,
Phil Hodkinson, Flora J. Macleod
and Ivor F. Goodson

with Norma Adair, Geoff Ford, Ruth Hawthorne,
Heather Hodkinson, Paul Lambe, Heather Lynch,
Irene Malcolm and Michael Tedder

 Routledge
Taylor & Francis Group

LONDON AND NEW YORK

First published 2011
by Routledge
2 Park Square, Milton Park, Abingdon, Oxon OX14 4RN

Simultaneously published in the USA and Canada
by Routledge
711 Third Avenue, New York, NY 10017

*Routledge is an imprint of the Taylor & Francis Group, an informa business*

© 2011 Gert J. J. Biesta, John Field, Phil Hodkinson, Flora J. Macleod and
Ivor F. Goodson

The right of the authors to be identified as the authors of this work has been
asserted by them in accordance with sections 77 and 78 of the Copyright,
Designs and Patents Act 1988.

Typeset in Charter and Stone Sans by
HWA Text and Data Management, London
Printed and bound in Great Britain by
CPI Antony Rowe, Chippenham, Wiltshire

*British Library Cataloguing in Publication Data*
A catalogue record for this book is available from the British Library

*Library of Congress Cataloging-in-Publication Data*
Improving learning through the lifecourse : learning lives / Gert J. J. Biesta
... [et al.]. – 1st ed.
      p. cm.
   Includes bibliographical references and index.
   1. Adult learning – Evaluation. 2. Adult education.
   3. Continuing education. 4. Career education. I. Biesta, Gert.
   LC5219.I486 2011
   374–dc22                                               2010039105

ISBN13: 978-0-415-57372-6 (hbk)
ISBN13: 978-0-415-57373-3 (pbk)
ISBN13: 978-0-203-82864-9 (ebk)

*For Martin Bloomer (1947–2002)*

# Contents

# Series editor's foreword

The Improving Learning series showcases findings from projects within UK Economic and Social Research Council's (ESRC's) Teaching and Learning Research Programme (TLRP) – the UK's largest ever coordinated educational research initiative.

Books in the Improving Learning series are explicitly designed to support 'evidence-informed' decisions in educational practice and policy-making. In particular, they combine rigorous social and educational science with high awareness of the significance of the issue being researched.

Working closely with practitioners, organisations and agencies covering all educational sectors, the Programme has supported many of the UK's best researchers to work on the direct improvement of policy and practice to support learning. Over 60 projects have been supported, covering many issues across the lifecourse. We are proud to present the results of this work through books in the Improving Learning series.

Each book provides a concise, accessible and definitive overview of innovative findings from TLRP investment. If more advanced information is required, the books may be used as a gateway to academic journals, monographs, websites, etc. On the other hand, shorter summaries and research briefings on key findings are also available via the programme's website at www.tlrp.org.

We hope that you will find the analysis and findings presented in this book are helpful to you in your work on improving outcomes for learners.

Andrew Pollard
Director, Teaching and Learning Research Programme
Institute of Education, University of London

# Preface

This book is based on the Learning Lives project that ran from 2004 to 2008 as part of the Teaching and Learning Research Programme overseen by the UK Economic and Social Research Council (Reference RES-139-25-0111). The project brought together a number of distinctive ideas, perspectives and people in order to engage with the question what learning 'means' and 'does' in the lives of adults. The Learning Lives project was unique in its scope and scale and in its ambition to combined longitudinal lifecourse and life-history data with data from large scale survey research.

This book is intended to provide a 'gateway' into the project rather than a fully comprehensive account of it. This has given us some difficult decisions about what to include and what to leave out. One immediately apparent effect is that we have only been able to represent a small proportion of the extensive and rich lifecourse and life-history data we collected in the project. More detailed accounts can be found in other publications from the project to which we refer throughout the chapters, as well as in the summative working papers listed on our website (www.learninglives.org).

The Learning Lives project was a collaboration between the Universities of Exeter, Stirling, Leeds and Brighton. The project was initiated by Martin Bloomer who sadly died in November 2002. His vision and commitment have played a crucial role in the development of the Learning Lives project. We are also indebted to the research fellows who worked on the project: Norma Adair, Geoff Ford, Ruth Hawthorne, Heather Hodkinson, Paul Lambe, Heather Lynch, Irene Malcolm and Michael Tedder.

July 2010
Gert J. J. Biesta, John Field, Phil Hodkinson,
Flora J. Macleod and Ivor F. Goodson

# Acknowledgements

We would like to thank all members of the project team for their help in bringing this book to fruition. We are also immensely grateful to the participants in the research for their willingness to share their stories and insights with us. Hilary Olek, the project administrator, deserves particular praise for her organisational contribution to the project. The Teaching and Learning Research Programme provided a series of challenges, opportunities and encouragements, and we would particularly like to thank Andrew Pollard and Miriam David for their support.

# Part I

# What are the issues?

# Chapter 1

# Learning, identity and agency in the lifecourse

This book is about the learning that goes on throughout adult life. Part of that learning is highly structured and takes place in taught courses of various kinds. Such courses might be held at a college, an adult education centre or a training facility, or they might be organised in the workplace or the offices of a voluntary organisation. Some are organised at a distance, so that people can study at home, at work or on the bus. A great deal of learning, however, takes place in what is often called 'the university of life'. We learn by doing something in a new way, by speaking to others, by reading something, or by watching other people. Increasingly people use new technologies to support their learning, whether it is highly formal and structured, or very informal and unplanned.

Adult learning has been widely studied from many perspectives. It is right that this is so, since adult learning is becoming increasingly important for a number of economic, social and policy reasons. We have set out in this book to look specifically at the role of learning throughout the lifecourse, focusing particularly on the role learning plays in the ways in which people make sense of and engage with changes in their lives. We look at the connections between learning and people's *identity* (who we think we are), as well as the ways that learning relates to *agency* (the ways in which people aim to shape their lives), always taking a lifecourse perspective on learning and its many contexts and purposes.

Our evidence is drawn from the Learning Lives project, a three-year, longitudinal, mixed-methods study into the learning biographies and trajectories of adults. In the remainder of this chapter we set out the wider scene, introduce the project, explain its design and methodology, and provide a brief overview of our findings. In the chapters that follow we present and discuss our findings in more details. Finally, as we are concerned with identifying the practical and policy implications of our research, we propose what we hope are innovative and creative ways in which people can be supported in learning throughout the lifecourse.

## The changing landscape of lifelong learning

Adult learning matters. There is now widespread agreement that modern countries like Britain depend largely on the creativity, skills and knowledge of the entire population, rather than on dwindling resources such as raw materials or a supply of people willing to work for very low wages. Many people talk of our future well-being in terms of a 'knowledge economy' and a 'learning society', in which every person's ability to develop new capabilities will provide them, and the wider community, with resources that will help them adapt and thrive. In practice, though, this broad agenda for learning is too easily reduced to a narrowly economic conception. As Peter Jarvis puts it: 'The lifelong learning society has become part of the current economic and political discourse of global capitalism, which positions people as human resources to be developed through lifelong learning, or discarded and retrained if their job is redundant' (Jarvis 2000, quoted in Grace 2004: 398). Or in the words of former UK Prime Minister Tony Blair: 'Education is the best economic policy we have' (Blair 1998, quoted in Martin 2002: 567).

Things do not have to be this way. Policy makers have, in the recent past, shown themselves willing to embrace a broad and generous view of learning in adult life. In 1972 the United Nations Educational, Scientific and Cultural Organization (UNESCO) published a landmark report on lifelong education. This report, entitled *Learning to be,* is remarkable because of the strength and breath of its vision about the significance of education throughout the lifecourse. The authors of the report speak about 'the fundamental solidarity of governments and of people', about a 'belief in democracy, conceived of as implying each man's right to realize his own potential and to share in the building of his own future', about 'the complete fulfilment of man, in all the richness of his personality', and argue that 'only an over-all, lifelong education can produce the kind of complete man the need for whom is increasing with the continually more stringent constraints tearing the individual asunder' (Faure et al. 1972: v–vi). The authors see the ultimate aim of education as '*to enable man to be himself, to "become himself"*' (Faure et al. 1972: xxxi; emphasis in original). For this, they argue that we need to learn 'how to build up a continually evolving body of knowledge all through life – "learn to be"' (Faure et al. 1972: vi).

*Learning to be* is also remarkable because its views stand in such sharp contrast to the policies and practices that dominate the 'new educational order' (Field 2006) of lifelong learning today. Exactly 25 years after the publication of *Learning to be* the Organisation for Economic Co-operation and Development (OECD) issued its own report on lifelong learning, *Lifelong learning for all* (OECD 1997). In contrast to *Learning to Be,* the OECD emphasised the economic rationale for lifelong learning. It presented the idea of 'lifelong learning for all' as the guiding principle for policy strategies 'that will respond directly to the need to improve the capacity of individuals, families, workplaces and communities to continuously adapt and renew' (OECD 1997: 3). According to *Lifelong learning for all*, the disappearance of many unskilled jobs, the more rapid turnover of products and services, and the fact that people change jobs more often than previously, all point to the need for 'more frequent renewal of knowledge and skills' (OECD 1997: 13). Lifelong learning 'from early childhood education to active learning in retirement' will thus be 'an important factor in promoting employment and economic development' (OECD 1997: 13).

What these documents show is that in about 25 years the focus of the discourse on lifelong learning appears to have shifted from 'learning to be' to 'learning to be productive and employable' (Biesta 2006; see also Boshier 1998, Field 2006). It appears to have shifted from lifelong learning as a means for personal development and social progress to lifelong learning as a means for economic growth and global competitiveness.

This is not merely a matter of definition but can have a real impact on the opportunities for people to engage in different forms of learning throughout their lives. Think, for example, of the way in which learning for personal development has been reclassified as 'leisure learning' and how, as a result, the opportunities to obtain public funding for such forms of learning have significantly decreased. The shift from 'learning to be' to 'learning to be productive and employable' can thus be read as a struggle over the definition of what counts as lifelong learning and, more importantly, about what counts as *worthwhile* lifelong learning.

The parameters of the current landscape of lifelong learning are also important from the perspective of research. Prevailing policy definitions of what counts as good or worthwhile learning tend to steer research agendas into particular directions so that other conceptions and practices of lifelong learning run the risk of disappearing from the radar. Thus much research tends to focus on lifelong learning as it occurs in institutional settings such as schools, colleges, community centres or the workplace, and on the evaluation of specific lifelong learning policies and practices. There is, however, much more to lifelong learning than this. The ambition of the Learning Lives project has precisely been to take a wider perspective on learning through the lifecourse, focusing on individual biographies and trajectories in order to gain an understanding of what learning – understood in the widest possible sense – 'means' and 'does' in the lives of adults.

## The Learning Lives project: learning, identity and agency in the lifecourse

The Learning Lives project was announced in the autumn of 2003 as part of the third phase of the Teaching and Learning Research Programme

(TLRP), a large programme of educational research managed by the UK's Economic and Social Research Council (ESRC). The project started in 2004 and finished in 2008. The overall aim of the project was to deepen understanding of the complexities of learning in the lifecourse whilst identifying, implementing and evaluating strategies for sustained positive impact upon learning opportunities, dispositions and practices, and upon the empowerment of adults. For this we were particularly interested in the interrelationships between learning, identity and agency in the lifecourse. To meet this aim we adopted a relatively complex, large-scale research design that combined life-history research, interpretative lifecourse research and quantitative survey research. The project was conducted in a partnership of researchers from four UK universities: Exeter, Brighton, Leeds and Stirling.

## Researching learning, identity and agency in the lifecourse

The main focus of the Learning Lives project was on the interrelationships between learning, identity and agency in the lifecourse. On the one hand we sought to understand how identity (including one's identity as a learner) and agency (seen as the ability to exert control over one's life) impact upon learning dispositions, practices and achievements. On the other hand we sought to understand how different forms and practices of learning and different learning achievements impact upon individual identities (including learner identities), on individuals' senses of agency and on their actual capacity to exert control over their lives.

We examined the meaning, significance and impact of a range of formal, informal, tacit and incidental learning events in the lives of adults. More importantly, we did so against the background of their unfolding lives as we aimed to understand the *transformations* in learning dispositions, practices and achievements that were triggered by *changes* occurring in the lifecourse. The unit of analysis in our project was therefore the *learning biography* (see Dominicé 2000).

For the purposes of the project we saw learning as having to do with the ways in which individuals *respond* to events in their lives, often in order to gain control over aspects of their lives (see Alheit 1994; Ranson et al. 1996; Antikainen et al. 1996; Biesta 2004). Such responses might take a number of quite different forms, ranging from adaptive to more active, creative or generative forms of learning. To understand learning in this way implies that it is seen as *contextually situated* (individuals interacting with and participating in their social and cultural milieu) and as having a *history* (both the individual's life history and the history of the practices and institutions in and through which learning takes place).

The events to which individuals respond and which may – but not necessarily always do – involve learning may be *structured* transitions or they may be changes of a more *incidental* nature, including critical incidents such as redeployment or illness. Many such events stimulate encounters with new formal and informal learning opportunities. They can also result in forms of tacit learning of which individuals sometimes only become aware (long) after the event. Learning also occurs, however, in relation to the routines of everyday life, where 'turning points' (Strauss 1962) are not immediately discernible.

Both *time* and *context* played a central role in what we aimed to achieve. Context is important because we hold that learning is about more than cognitive processes happening inside the mind. In our view learning is inextricably related to doing and being, which is why we needed to approach what and how people learn through an understanding of the contexts in which and, more importantly, the practices *through* which they learn (see Hodkinson et al. 2007, 2008a). Since learning always involves the reworking of earlier experiences and because in many cases people engage in learning in order to bring about future change, learning also needs to be understood in its temporal dimension. In our project, the temporal perspective is essential for two further reasons: first because of our interest in the interrelationships between learning and life (the learning biography); and second because the contexts in and through which people learn are themselves not static but subject to change and transformation (for examples in the way in which available opportunities for learning change over time see Antikainen et al. 1996; Gorard and Rees 2002). This, in turn, means that contexts matter at two levels: the immediate contexts in and through which adults learn, and the changing contexts that form the 'backdrop' of their learning biographies.

There were, therefore, three challenges for our research. How can we investigate learning over time? How can we investigate the contexts of such learning? And how can we investigate the temporality of such contexts? We addressed these challenges through a combination of two forms of longitudinal research: life-history research and lifecourse research. The retrospective understanding of the learning biography is the main aim of *life-history research* while the real time 'tracking' of the ways in which learning biographies are 'lived' and evolve over time is the main object of longitudinal *lifecourse research*.

Several studies have utilised these approaches for understanding the learning of (young) adults from a temporal point of view. Most of them, however, have either used a retrospective *or* a real-time approach, but not a combination of both (examples of the first are Antikainen et al. 1996; Gorard and Rees 2002; examples of the latter are Hodkinson et al. 1996; Ball et al. 2000). The reason for combining the two approaches was not only that it increases the time span available for investigation. It was also because each approach can add depth to the interpretation of data generated through the other approach. Each, in other words, is a potential source for contextualising and interpreting the findings of the other (see below).

## Project design

In the project we combined life-history research with two different forms of lifecourse research: longitudinal interpretative lifecourse research and quantitative survey research. The first two approaches used interviews for data collection. Over a period of 36 months we conducted 528 interviews with 117 people, 59 male and 58 female, aged between 25 and 84 at first interview. Most interviews lasted for about two hours. The average number of interviews per individual was four to five (for more information, see the methodological appendix at the end of this book). Rather than conducting our own survey we analysed data from the British Household Panel Survey (BHPS), an annual panel survey of each adult member of a nationally representative sample of 5,500 British households first recruited in 1991, contained about 10,000 individuals (Institute for Social and Economic Research 2010).

We used the BHPS to develop an understanding of patterns of formal part-time education and training during adulthood (our dependent variable). Our independent variables were age, gender, cohort (generation group), place (UK nation-state), social class, occupational status, household tenure, disability (objective and subjective), employment status, income status, marital status, parenthood and family status. We used a number of variables to study family background and inter-generational influences. The longitudinal structure of the BHPS made it possible to follow individuals over time and develop an understanding of changes in the patterns and predictors of participation and non-participation in formal education and training. The analytical advantages of using longitudinal data were the ability to study patterns, trends and dynamics of participation by focusing on individual change over time; study transitions between states of participation and non-participation, what triggered the change including the timing of a change of state in relation to other transitions and events; study individual specific effects on patterns of participation; and study the effects of events (natural interventions and imposed interventions such as policy change).

In the interviews, we focused initially on the life history. We started by asking participants the question: 'Can you tell me about your life?' Subsequent interviews increasingly focused on ongoing events in the lives of participants. Interviewers took an open approach, asking for clarification and elaboration, with progressive focusing on key project interests and themes. In the final interview participants were asked about their experiences of taking part in the project. All interviews were recorded, transcribed and checked by the interviewer. Transcripts were made available to the participants but they were not required to read or check them. Building on our experience with the analysis of large, qualitative data sets (Hodkinson et al. 2005; James and Biesta 2007), we developed an approach that suited the logistics and objectives of the project. After each interview interviewers wrote short memos capturing salient experiences and early interpretations. Over time these developed into substantive records of ongoing analysis. We used two approaches for systematic data analysis in an iterative relationship. *Thematic analysis* focused on larger numbers of cases around particular themes, using both theoretically driven analysis and data-driven analysis. *Biographical analysis* focused on the in-depth analysis of individuals and resulted in the construction of detailed individual case studies.

We were guided by the research ethics code of the British Educational Research Association. We ensured that participants understood the nature of the research and that they were aware that they could withdraw from the project at any time. We asked for signed consent for participation and separate signed consent for making transcripts available for future research. Participants used self-chosen pseudonyms except where they decided to use their own names. We omitted sensitive data where we judged that publication might be harmful to participants and anonymised background data in order to protect participants from possible recognition. In those cases where we felt that relationships were developing beyond research relationships we made participants aware of opportunities for help and support.

## Methodology: combining life-history and interpretative lifecourse research

It may seem that life history and lifecourse research can easily be combined, in that one approach deals with the past and the other with the ongoing present, so that together they can seamlessly cover the whole lifespan or at least major parts of it. The relationship between the two approaches is, however, more complicated and more interesting than this, particularly because our understanding of the present influences our account of the past just as our understanding of the past influences our account of the present.

Life-history research relies on the ways in which adults are able to reconstruct their past through the narration of their life story. Such stories are not an objective account of the facts of one's life. Life stories are 'lives interpreted and made textual' and should therefore be seen as 'a partial, selective commentary on lived experience' (Goodson and Sikes 2001: 16). Life-history research does not study lives themselves but rather '*texts of lives*' (Freeman 1998: 7, quoted in Goodson and Sikes 2001: 16). Given that the life story is the *current* interpretation of one's past, the way in which a life is storied and narrated will crucially depend on the present. The 'now' is, in other words, always present in one's story of the past. This is not to say that each different 'now' will produce a completely different life story. But people do adjust their interpretation and evaluation of their past in the light of new experiences. Current success, for example, may lead to a quite different account of one's past than current failure. It is for this reason that life-history research needs to have an understanding of the situation from which the past is reconstructed and narrated. While good life-history research will take the importance of the present into account, lifecourse research with its emphasis on understanding the ongoing present can add significantly to the understanding of the position from which the life story is being told.

It is not just the present *situation* that influences one's understanding of the past. The way in which people *understand and articulate* their present situation is important as well. It is, in other words, not just the 'now' that is always present in one's story of the past; it is also one's *story of the 'now'* that impacts on one's story of the past. This is where interpretative lifecourse research can add even more to a life history approach, because of its emphasis on understanding the ongoing present. Interpretative lifecourse research cannot claim to be more objective than life-history research, because both have to deal with 'lives interpreted and made textual'. But through its detailed understanding of the stories people tell about their ongoing lives, it can contribute to a better grasp of how such stories and current ways of understanding impact on how people make sense of and story their past.

Just as the present and our understanding of the present influence our stories and interpretations of the past, the past also impacts on the present. Although we do not want to espouse determinism and are aware that life is characterised both by continuity and discontinuity, past events do both enable and restrict our opportunities to act in the present. In this respect we can say that the past is present in the 'now'. But again it is not only the way in which the past enables and restricts what is possible in the present that is important. The past also influences our *understanding* of the present and our ability to articulate and narrate the present, just as our stories of our past and our ability to make sense of our past influence the present and the stories we tell of it. This is where life-history research can add significantly to the real-time understanding generated by lifecourse research, in that it can help to understand the past and the ways in which people's understanding of the past impact on the present.

For all these reasons we cannot simply think of the combination of life-history and interpretative life-course research as a process in which one approach deals with the past and the other with the ongoing present. Since both approaches are forms of interpretative research that have the interpretations adults give of their lives as their object of study, past and present do not exist objectively and separately but constantly interpenetrate each other. The present and our stories of the present influence our stories of the past, the past influences the present and our stories of the present, just as our stories of the past influence the present and our stories of the present.

One further complicating factor has to do with the impact of the research process itself on the ways in which lives are narrated and interpreted. Engaging in life-history and lifecourse interviews is likely to result in a more active and reflexive relationship with one's past and current life. This may impact on the way in which participants understand, interpret and narrate their lives, in that participation in the research process is likely to create a heightened awareness of one's life. It may also impact on the lives themselves. While such impact may be beneficial – some life-history work with adults is precisely aimed at using the approach to influence the lives of participants in a positive way (see Dominicé 2000) – we shouldn't deny the fact that telling the story of one's past and present life can be a difficult and in some cases even a traumatic experience (West 1996).

## A summary of our main findings

In the following chapters we engage in detail with the main findings from our research. In this section we provide a brief overview of some of the key insights that we gained from the research. One important distinction in the presentation of findings is that between learning through the lifecourse and learning *from* the lifecourse. Part of our findings focuses on how learning occurs at different ages and stages of people's lives, but our research has also generated detailed understanding of the ways in which life itself can be an object of learning and understanding.

### The ubiquity of learning

A major finding is that learning of some sort is ubiquitous in people's lives. Though hardly surprising, our research has not only generated extensive fine-grained longitudinal evidence of the variety, scope, characteristics and trajectories of learning in the lifecourse, but has also provided empirical support for our assumption that learning 'means' and 'does' much more in the lives of adults than what is often emphasised in current policy. In this regard the research provides a strong argument for the need to take a broad and encompassing view about the meaning and significance of learning through the lifecourse.

### Learning through the lifecourse

The research has generated detailed evidence of the ubiquity and variety of learning in adults' lives. We have found that much learning is tacit and routinised, but also that major life-changing events often trigger learning, just as learning can lead to significant changes in people's lives. We have found that adults have widely differing dispositions towards learning. For many, learning is merely a fact of life, closely connected to their continual striving to deal with everyday problems, rather than viewing it as occurring as learning per se. For a minority, though, the sense of being a learner is an important part of their identity. In some cases this learner identity is focused around formal education but always with substantial informal learning related to it.

Learning is sometimes valued for the outcomes it brings, but people often value the process of engagement in learning for its own sake. Judgements about what counts as good or worthwhile learning differ significantly and the judgements of individuals may be at odds with official policy, which can impact negatively on adults' opportunities to learn what is important to them. Learning is not necessarily a positive experience and does not necessarily have positive outcomes. Progression and transitions in people's lives, such as retirement, can valuably be understood as learning processes. Especially within education and employment there are significant barriers to progression for some people.

## Engagement with part-time education and training

Analysis of qualitative data identified two types of engagement with part-time education and training. Some participation involved low levels of involvement, with little impact upon identity. Some adults develop a high level of involvement, where being a learner/student becomes an important part of their life and sense of self. It is this high level involvement that can lead to personal change, including the achievement of agency (see below). For those people, participation in part-time education and training is a long-term process, not a 'quick fix'.

Analysis of BHPS data gave us a detailed empirical understanding of participation in part-time education and training, of the factors influencing such participation and of trajectories of participation over time. We found that in most cases, participation in part-time education and training did not result in a higher level qualification. We found stronger gender effects than commonly reported in cross-sectional research (e.g. Tuckett and Aldridge 2010), particularly amongst the younger cohorts studied, although young women who made an early transition into parenthood had a higher probability than any of their contemporaries of returning to formal education and training later on in their lives. We found a marked age effect, strongly suggesting that almost everybody stops participating in formal education and training by the age of 55. We found that participation patterns were influenced (a) by prior learning and employment, including the nature of that employment in terms of the manual/non-manual divide; (b) by externally imposed events in people's lives as well as the choices they made, including the timing of these events and choices in the lifecourse; and (c) by one's social class status at age fourteen and – as in Gorard and Rees' Welsh data (2002) – by mothers' and fathers' education and work histories.

### Learning from life through narrative and narration

The project has generated detailed evidence of ways in which adults learn *from* their lives. The life-history methodology has helped us to explore the significance of narrative and narration in such learning processes, something we have captured in the idea of 'narrative learning'. We have found that stories and storying are important vehicles for learning from one's life and we have been able to show how differences in the 'narrative quality' of life stories (narrative intensity; descriptive–evaluative; plot and emplotment; flexibility) correlate with different learning *processes* ('learning potential' of life stories) and differing learning *outcomes* ('action potential'). We have found important differences in the efficacy of life storying and have been able to establish relationships between styles of narration, forms of narrative learning and agency.

We have found that the 'capacity' to learn from one's life is not necessarily fixed but can itself be learned. Life stories play a crucial role in the articulation of a sense of self, which means that narrative learning can be seen as a form of 'identity work'. Narrative learning operates at the intersection of 'internal conversations' and social practices of storytelling, which means that for many the social opportunities for narrating one's life story are an important vehicle for narrative learning and an important avenue for improving the capacity for narrative learning.

### Learning and identity

In the research we have taken identity as having to do with one's sense of self. We have theorised this more specifically in terms of the dispositions people have towards themselves, life and learning. We found that dispositions together with positions can both enable and constrain learning. Many aspects of the sense of self remain implicit but can become more explicit at times of change and crisis; however, this is not necessarily the case, as particular dispositions and a particular sense of self may also prevent learning and change, even through times of crisis. The narration of one's life story is not only an important vehicle for expressing one's sense of self, but also for articulating and actively constructing such a sense of self. Relationships between identity and learning often become clear at times of crisis and change. When people go through major life-changing events they are often presented by a need to learn. Learning can then contribute to changes in some dispositions, and thus a person's identity. It is, however, possible that existing dispositions are so strong that learning and subsequent change in identity do not happen. Our data suggest a widespread 'need' for the construction of a (coherent) life story that helps individuals to make sense and come to terms with their life and adjust to changes in their lives.

## *Learning and agency*

We have taken agency to be about the ability to give direction to one's life. This ability is, we found, always situated in specific circumstances and relationships. We have found that learning itself may or may not be agentically driven: it can be self-initiated or forced by others or be incidental. Learning may result in increase or decrease of agency. Increased agency seems to be more obvious and common, but much depends on the extent to which people acknowledge that they have learned something. This is more obvious in relation to formal education and training, often because qualifications open up new possibilities for action. Experiences of successful learning also impact positively on people's self-confidence, which in turn can lead to increased agency in many aspects of their lives. The research indicates that the extent to which learning 'translates' into agency depends on a range of factors and also on the particular 'ecological' conditions of people's field of action. Decreased agency through learning occurs when people learn that things are too difficult or that they cannot cope, which, in turn, impacts upon their sense of self.

## Outline of the book

In the chapters that follow we present our findings in more detail. Given the sheer size and scale of the Learning Lives project we have chosen to focus the discussion on a number of key themes and areas. In Chapter 2 we look at the role of informal learning through the lifecourse. Chapter 3 discusses formal education and training. In Chapter 4 we explore the ways in which people can learn from their lives through narrative and narration. Chapter 5 focuses on the role of generations in learning through the lifecourse. In Chapter 6 we explore the role of positions and dispositions in understanding the relationship between learning, identity and agency in the lifecourse. In the final chapter of the book we ask what the research suggests for the improvement of learning through the lifecourse. And in the appendix we provide more detailed information about the design, methodology and methods of the research.

As we showed earlier in this chapter, lifelong learning is currently at the centre of many policies and initiatives, nationally and internationally. While this may be good news for educators and educationalists who wish to promote lifelong learning, and also for those who wish to be actively engaged in learning throughout their lives, there is an obvious risk that policies will influence ideas about what counts as good or worthwhile lifelong learning. Our study shows that people seek meaning through learning in a range of ways across their lives, but often in circumstances that are constrained and influenced by forces that they do not control. We need to explore and understand these forces, as well as the diverse and complex meanings of learning in people's lives, if we are to improve opportunities for learning through the lifecourse.

# Part 2

## What does the research tell us?

# Chapter 2

# Informal learning

## Introduction

All of us learn, all of the time. This is pretty much a statement of the obvious. Much learning takes place in formal settings such as colleges, universities or community education centres. Even in these circumstances, though, people are also engaged in informal learning. What is often termed informal learning is a ubiquitous part of living. Such informal learning arises mainly out of the experiences of living. It can be significant or insignificant, intended or unintended, and transformative or trivial. Much is often tacit and unrecognised as learning, even by those concerned. Much writing on informal learning has portrayed it as separate and qualitatively different from formal learning. Yet as Colley et al. have argued, it makes sense to see formality and informality as attributes of almost all learning situations (Colley et al. 2003: 20–21; see also Straka 2004). We recognise that there is a risk that we too may seem to pull formal and informal learning apart, simply by virtue of devoting separate chapters to analysing how people learn formally and informally throughout their lives. But that is not our intention. People learn informally while involved in the most formal settings, and sometimes what they learn runs counter to the stated intentions of the institution. Daisy Paterson, daughter of a miner and factory worker from the west of Scotland, learned how to 'play the actress', pretending to be ill so as to avoid a primary school where she was rapped across the hand with a ruler for being behind children who came from more middle class families. Formal and informal learning are inevitably interwoven throughout the lifecourse; what is important is what the learning means to people, and what it does in their lives.

We start this chapter with some comments on recent theories of learning. These help to place our discussion of informal learning in a broader conceptual context. We then go on to examine several people's stories of the role of informal learning in their lives. One aspect of informal learning is its role in the workplace, which tends to attract the attention of policy makers, whose interest lies in the identification and accreditation of informal learning as a way of building the skills and capacities of the workforce. In the European Union, for example, the Council agreed in 2004 to a resolution approving common principles for 'the identification and validation of non-formal and informal learning', leading to publication in 2009 of standardised guidelines for assessing informal learning, as part of the emerging European Qualifications Framework (CEDEFOP 2009). We therefore conclude the chapter with some remarks on the feasibility of this policy effort.

## Theories of learning

In recent years, established theories of learning have come under attack. These controversies derive from different ways of understanding learning. Sfard (1998) has argued that we can understand different understandings of learning by looking at the metaphors that people use. Until recently, she suggests, the dominant model was represented through the term *acquisition*. That is to say, knowledge, understanding or skills are known quantities, and when people learn, they are simply acquiring these from elsewhere – a teacher, a text or another authority. This is, she emphasises, certainly one valid way of understanding some learning. In our stories, there are plenty of examples of people acquiring pre-existing skills and knowledge. Sfard's point is that it is simply one way of understanding a complex activity like learning, but it is not the only possible way in which learning can be captured or understood.

Why is the acquisition metaphor not enough? The first problem is that it is often used in ways that portray learning as a one-off event (see Hodkinson 2005; Hager 2005). A particular skill or piece of knowledge is set as a goal, it is taught and acquired, and that is the end of the event; if more is needed, it is followed by another acquisition event, and so on. Yet learning appears to be a continuing and iterative process, rather than an identifiable single event. Related to this, the acquisition metaphor is also used in ways that separate out the learner, the process of learning, and the content of what is learned. That is to say, it treats the content as separate and independent from the learner and the learning process. We know that this can often be the case, as for example when someone learns the basic rules of driving, or a set of skills needed to lay bricks, or a set of historical dates. In behaviourist terms, then, what is needed is for the learner to acquire these skills and then use them. The skills or knowledge remain unaffected and timeless; the educational question is about the most efficient way of transferring them to the learner.

Behaviourist ideas have been extremely influential in British policy thinking about adult learning and skills for many years (Field 2007), influencing the development of standards-led approaches to professional and vocational learning. This has resulted in a 'technical-efficiency' view of learning that characterised much British policy in the domain of skills and qualifications under New Labour. Yet, as many of our stories show, both the processes and content of learning are essentially social in nature. Tony Wilf, a man in his fifties who would usually be described as an unskilled manual worker, learned how to make and repair roads as a member of a road gang. As he tells it, his learning cannot be separated from his identity and position. To take one example, Tony started off working alongside 'a pothole man'.

> I mean, the first day I went, I had no idea. You know, I knew basically how to shovel, or I thought I did, you know. But ... you got the people showing me how to make the shovel work for you, not you work for the shovel. And from there you sort of progressed. You could go with another gang where they'd do big road construction or they'd do footpaths.

And so he learned different aspects of the work as a member of the road gang, at the same time exemplifying and strengthening his position and identity as a member of a male working class community.

Sfard's second metaphor is that of *participation*, which she sees as characteristic of much recent writing about learning. She notes that in such theories as situated learning and activity theory, knowledge is mentioned rarely, and the emphasis is rather on the activity of knowing (Sfard 1998: 6). Lave and Wenger's book (1991) on situated learning has been particularly influential in this regard (see Lang and Canning 2010). In their work they focus on learning as a dimension of social participation. In their model, learning takes place when people join a community of practice; as novices, they are on the fringes of the community, where their position as novice means that they are constantly testing and reflecting on their actions and interactions with more experienced members. Over time, the novice becomes expert, and in turn helps other, newer members to build their knowledge and skills. The concept of 'legitimate peripheral participation' plays a key role in this theory.

According to Wenger (1998), learning in any community of practice can occur in four domains. He defines these as meaning (learning as experience), practice (learning as doing), community (learning as belonging) and identity (learning as becoming). Through participation, then, learners are placed in a position where they learn cognitively, emotionally, socially and physically. For Wenger, this process alters our sense of our selves and our capacities, leading him to write of the 'transformative practice of a learning community' (Wenger 1998: 215). Specific settings – that is to say, particular communities of practice – thus form what Wenger calls 'social ecologies of identity' (Wenger 1998: 211). Given our interest in identity and learning, we are particularly interested in Wenger's conclusion that 'membership in a community of practice translates into identity as a form of competence' (Wenger 1998: 153).

In the case of Tony Wilf, membership of a community of practice was both empowering and limiting. He acquired a number of skills as a member of the road gang, even though he was formally an unskilled labourer. As well as learning particular road repair and building skills, he also learned to drive a mobile compressor and then a roller, taking part in a combination of formal training (for the roller) and informal learning by participating in the gang's activities. His membership of the gang was enormously important to him:

> The bunch of lads that you worked with were brilliant. I mean you could work all over the city and so you always got different surroundings... You never felt hard done by because you were always laughing and joking.

He learned from more experienced men who he respected, when he developed the skills to deal with potholes or drive the compressor. When he learned paving and masonry, though, he was not allowed to apply the skills, because he had developed them solely through informal learning. As he told it, 'basic reason I didn't get proper street mason pavier's thing, is because you'd go to college, and you'd to do all the – the measurement'. The issue is that Tony's literacy and numeracy skills were basic. This also limited his role in other ways, leading him to avoid jobs where he had to record measurements or fill out forms. Yet informal learning had been a rich part of his working life, enabling him to build a more varied and fulfilling working life than is suggested by the phrase 'unskilled labour', and giving him a strong and secure sense of belonging in a community that he also helped to construct.

This brings us to a third metaphor for learning, learning as *construction*. Constructivist views of learning focus on the ways in which learners build their own skills and knowledge, as part of a process of making sense of, and coming to own, what they are learning. Constructivist notions of the learner as an active builder of meaning and knowledge have a long history in educational thinking. Conceptually, constructivism is distinct from (though often confused with) constructionist theories, which insist that reality is a construct, and are therefore relativist. For example, a constructionist would claim that the physical world is what a learner makes of it; a constructivist approach would recognise the creative and imaginary contribution of physicists to our understanding of particle physics, while accepting that there is plenty of evidence that the subatomic constituents of matter have an existence independent of our knowledge of them. Similarly, while laying pavement slabs involves some processes and techniques that are valid in any circumstances, Tony Wilf nevertheless learned the skills of pavement laying in a particular context, and attached particular meanings to his involvement in that context.

There have been many different views on learning as a process of construction. In his later work, the educational psychologist Jean Piaget (1952) suggested that learners construct new knowledge from their experiences through processes of accommodation and assimilation; he took a radically individual approach to learning, seeing it as the self-referential activity of each individual brain. In this form, there are three serious weaknesses in construction as a metaphor for learning. First, particularly in its individualistic and Piagetian forms, learning is seen as almost entirely cognitive, concerned with brain/mind and with propositional knowledge. Construction is seen as a purely mental process; yet as we have seen with Tony's story, learning is always embodied, in ways that incorporate but are not limited to the brain. Practice was and is central to his learning, as are his emotions – what he felt in terms of affect as well as sensed through touch, sight, smell and hearing. Thinking, reflecting and enacting involve much more of the body than just the brain, and our learners' stories show the importance of the embodied, practical, sensory and affective dimensions of learning.

The second problem with much constructivist thinking on learning is that its focus is primarily on formal learning, such as school science or mathematics (Cobb and Bowers 1999). It set out to answer important questions about the difficulties apparently experienced by schoolchildren in studying science and mathematics, and how to tackle these obstacles to learning. This approach has had much less to say about informal learning, yet as Tony's story illustrates, many of our interviewees have led very rich, fulfilled lives while taking part in learning that is almost entirely informal. Even when Tony turned to formal learning in computing and basic skills, he hated and resisted anything that reminded him of 'going back to being like at high school'. Effective learning, for Tony, came when his tutor responded to him as an individual, and encouraged him to explore and write about the history of Quarry Hill, his local community.

Both of these objections to the constructivist metaphor can be handled if we view the learning process as socially embedded (as in the participation metaphor) and embodied. While radical constructivist approaches have largely followed Piaget's 'genetic individualism', situated cognition theories have tended to start with the Russian psychologist Lev Vygotsky, who pioneered a far more sociocultural approach to learning as construction (Daniels 2001: 37–39). A number of authors, such as Paul Hager (2005), have followed the American educational theorist John Dewey in exploring a constructivist theory of learning that recognises the embodied and social nature of learning, but is neither radically individualist or socially determinist. Dewey, who has been described as a 'transactional constructivist' (see Biesta and Burbules 2003), saw people as belonging to a 'common world', in which the co-construction of knowledge inevitably involved shared understanding and meaning, rather than the widely divergent individual stances envisaged by radical constructivist approaches, or the structurally socialised subjects of Vygotsky's cultural–historical constructivism. These insights help us understand Tony Wilf's learning as an embodied social process. Throughout his lifecourse to date, the negative experiences of school, work as learning, learning in and through the family, and in his later adult education courses, learning has been and continues to be a process of becoming.

There is a third problem with the constructivist metaphor that is harder to overcome. Like other accounts of learning grouped together by Sfard as 'acquisition', constructivist theory still tends to see learning as an event that takes place in a context. In its more extreme and radically individualist forms, contructivism has often presented the context not only as separated from the learning, but as something that can more or less be taken as a given, without further attention. These individualist approaches came under increasing attack during the late 1980s and the 1990s from a number of writers who drew on Vygotsky. Lave and Wenger (1991), Brown et al. (1989) and a growing number of post-Vygotskian researchers (Wertsch 1998; Engeström 1999) have examined ways in which learning varies in different situations. Learning, they argue, is always situated; and the situation is part of the learning, not something separated from it.

For Lave and Wenger, learning and its meanings are configured through the learner's attempts to become a full participant in a sociocultural practice. But this is not an isolated process, insulated from the social relations and material objects that happen to surround it. On the contrary, they argue that 'learning is not situated in practice – as if it were some independently reifiable process than just happened to be situated somewhere; learning is an integral part of generative social practice in the lived-in world' (Lave and Wenger 1991: 35). The nature of the social relationships involved not only influence and shape the learning, but are themselves part of a set of learning processes (Field and Spence 2000).

Tony's case shows how his work-based learning in his early adult life was centred within the participatory practices of the workplace. Much of it was informal learning. And it is very noticeable that much of the academic research on situated learning did not involve formal education or training programmes; most of it was based on studies of informal learning in workplaces, in voluntary organisations, or in the naturalistic settings of anthropological fieldwork. Where these theorists and researchers did engage with formal learning, it was often to present evidence that the school situation was organised in ways that produced the very pedagogic problems with science and mathematics that earlier, more Piagetian constructivists had focused on. These writers therefore merged constructivist approaches with others that viewed learning as participation (Rogoff 2003).

Such an approach offers considerable insight into the importance and nature of informal learning, as we have seen in the case of Tony Wilf. It does need, though, to be qualified in at least one essential way. A number of writers have noted that most theories of situated learning fail to address inequalities of power and authority (Tennant 1997; Field 2006). There may be situations where the community of practice is weak, and is unable to access the resources that are needed to support effectively processes of legitimate peripheral participation. Alternatively, the community of practice may be characterised by hierarchical power relationships that restrain – possibly intentionally – entry and participation. Educational entry qualifications often function as exclusionary mechanisms of this kind. Moreover, as Lave and Wenger accept, some writers have fallen into the trap of romanticizing communities of practice, failing to see how they can be used to advance the interests of particular groups or classes. Moreover, as Tennant (1997: 79) notes, there is also a tendency in their work to demonize formal education and training institutions, presenting tendencies towards testing and accreditation as examples of bureaucratic and professional control over learning, which they contrast with the free exchange of skills and knowledge that typify communities of practice. In later chapters, we draw on the work of Pierre Bourdieu to explore the ways in which inequalities of resources and position can shape learning. While recognising the potential of recent theories to help us understand informal learning, then, we need to bear in mind some of their limitations.

## Informality in learning

Looking at Tony Wilf's learning trajectory thus reminds us that informal and formal learning are artificial and rather arbitrary categories. In his fifties, Tony decided to return to formal education, with a view to helping his daughter with schoolwork. Initially, he joined a class called 'Computers for the terrified'. By this time, he had left the road gang as a result of an industrial injury, and was combining parenting (his wife had died) with a series of part-time jobs, 'ducking and diving' to keep things going. He picked up parenting skills by a process of trial and error, complemented by advice from neighbours and the children themselves. He saw himself now first and foremost as a father: 'I sort of like to think that I've sort of taken over from Liz with my kids and sort of say, "Right, you know, this is what we do."' But even these resources were not enough to enable him to run the home that he wanted, as he discovered when he asked a neighbour how to make batter, and she gave him a cookery book. The turning point came when he discovered that his daughter was diagnosed as severely dyslexic.

> Clare's handwriting – if I can't decipher it, nobody can decipher it. So I – the idea was to get a computer so she'd be able to do it and print it out. And so that's when it started. And I thought, 'Well, what do you do?'

Having then moved on to an English course, Tony found himself working, with his tutor's encouragement, on local history. This in turn had set him off on a new learning journey, drawing on websites and memories outside the course, while showing his writing to his tutor.

For Tony, intentional learning in adult life mostly entailed informal learning. He attended a small number of training courses, as when learning to drive a roller. Like several others in our study, he preferred informal learning, and when he returned to formal education he left a basic skills course in which he felt that the tutor was treating him in a way that reminded him of school. Fortunately, Tony had completed a basic computing course, which 'worked' for him, and knew that not all adult tutors were like this. This led him to try another course in a different centre, where he felt that the tutor treated him as an individual. So he certainly did not reject formal education and training. Rather, he looked for an approach in formal education that was – in our terms – as participatory and constructivist in its own way as the informal learning he had undertaken as a member of the road gang.

Derek Hutchinson tells a comparable story of informal learning. Born in 1944, much of his working life had been spent in the construction industry in West Yorkshire, sometimes as an employee, more often as a self-employed subcontractor. His family background was in building. He broke with the tradition only in training as a carpenter rather than following his male relations into bricklaying. He left school as early as he could, taking an apprenticeship based solely on workplace practice. At no time in his working life did he take a formal college course. He mainly built new skills by working on new types of site, including historic buildings, albeit that in 1975 he did take an in-house course on dry lining. He was made redundant, along with a number of others, when his company was taken over by another firm that placed a premium on formal qualifications. He then worked in a pub, before moving to a job as a driver, and is coping with the onset of arthritis. Given his health and age, he is looking ahead to retirement with mixed feelings.

Like Tony's, Derek's story is that of belonging to a strong community of practice. He trained and carried out much of his work in an environment dominated by very small firms, characterised by close relationships between the different employers and workmen, strong interpersonal loyalty and trust, and respect for the experience and skills of expert, skilled men. His hobbies show similarities to this. Derek is a philatelist and postcard collector, and has turned his pastime into a secondary business, building connections to a variety of others to whom he sells. He has run his local philately society, and has given lectures in the area for a number of years. He has a wide variety of contacts through this community. This interest in turn is related to another long-established interest, in local and family history, which he pursues through archival and online research. Having invested in a computer, he took a short course in IT at a local 'learndirect' centre (there was no qualification), and is now learning by a combination of leaflets, handbooks, trial and error and advice from his daughters and staff at his local computer shop. His intention is to use the computer to build up his business if his job as a driver comes to an end.

Derek has no particular dislike of formal education. On the contrary: both of his daughters are educated to third level and working in professional roles, and he is enormously proud of their achievements. He has also clearly learned considerably by informal means, at work, in the family and through his hobbies. Unlike Tony Wilf, though, learning appears to be central to Derek's sense of who he is. He speaks of new skills and knowledge as something he has always worked on, mostly 'through trial and error'. As the story unfolds, though, it shows someone who has learned himself and taught others by participation in several communities of practice, turning to others for advice and providing it to others in turn. There is no sharp watershed moment in the narrative, in contrast to Tony's realisation that he could and should be doing more to help his daughter following his wife's death and Clare's diagnosis as dyslexic. Rather, he has continued to learn throughout his life, and learning has been continually important to his sense of who he is, as a builder, father, philatelist, postcard collector and family historian. For Tony Wilf, on the other hand, it is a recent transformation.

## Informal learning in working life

For several of our interviewees, learning was triggered by turning points in working life. For some of the time, and for some people, this led to participation in a formal course, either provided by the employer or by an outside agency. Even in these cases, of course, participation in formal learning took place against the background of continuing informal learning, which was more or less reflexive in character. Informal learning was, as we have said, a constant through the lives of all our participants; but it was likely to become particularly significant at times of change, particularly if those changes questioned or challenged someone's existing identity or dispositions.

The Learning Lives project allowed us to explore these issues afresh. Unlike much research on workplace learning, which, understandably, focuses primarily upon the workforce or the training programme, we were able to look at things from the perspective of the person's learning life, and see workplace learning as one often important part of that. This entails the integration of two different dimensions. First, at any one time a person's learning in the workplace can be usefully understood as one part of their wider living and learning. Change and learning at work always run alongside and form an important element of developments in other areas of life such as the family, the neighbourhood, friendship networks, leisure activities and so on, including any participation in formal learning outside of work. Second, and related to this, workplace life and learning can usefully be seen within the longer perspective of the lifecourse. Working roles and contexts change over the course of one's life, sometimes dramatically, and the nature and significance of workplace learning can change with them. It is also important to see these transformations through the working life in their relationship to other changes in one's position and habitus throughout the lifecourse; for example, promotion and greater responsibility might come along just as your children reach a critical stage of their lives.

William Moore's life story neatly illustrates some of these issues. Born into a traditional mining community in the 1940s in Yorkshire, William's mother was a pillar of the community, active in the church, the Girl Guides and other local women's associations, while his father was a coalface worker in a local colliery. William won a place at his local grammar school. While his parents were agreed that their own children should not work in mining, they had little grasp of the education system, having left early themselves to enter the labour market. William found it a difficult environment, disrupting existing friendship networks and associations like the church youth club, so he put efforts into maintaining these ties, partly through football. He left school with a few qualifications, initially starting work in sales and marketing, which he then left to become a trainee textile designer. This required him to learn craft skills such as machine knitting, learning how each setting then created particular patterns. He also attended college courses, but saw them as less useful and valuable than the working experiences he was undertaking. He was then moved into the design room, where one of the more experienced men – John, whom William described as bearded and 'bohemian' – encouraged him to join a brass band. On completing this training, John and William (who had meanwhile married) set up their own design partnership.

The next major turning point for William was the break-up of both his marriage and the business partnership. Following a new girlfriend, who had a job in Barcelona, he moved to Spain, where his business thrived for a number of years. He learned both Spanish and Catalan, and adapted his design work to Spanish tastes, as well as adjusting to the impact of new technologies on the manufacturers who were his customers. He also joined a local dance band, playing trumpet at weddings and other local events. After ten years in Spain, the family returned to Britain, mainly for the sake of their sons' secondary education. This was also a time when European textile manufacturing was in decline, and in his late fifties William was losing custom. With a view to finding something else, he visited the job centre and took career guidance, which involved him learning how to write an attractive CV. He also took a computing course – the first formal education he had taken for many years. Then at 61 he found part-time work in a local music shop, which he enjoyed greatly, drawing as he did on his knowledge of music, and his ability to communicate effectively with customers; as some of the shop's business was overseas, he was also able to call on his language skills.

William described his approach to learning as typified by a preference for informality, practical experience and pragmatism. He found it difficult to separate out learning as a discrete activity.

> I tend to drift into things, and not realise that one is learning things, really, but I suppose when you look back on it, I obviously have learnt a lot of things through my life, but it's trying to find out, pick them out and say, 'Oh, yes, that was an actual learning experience', rather than just everything is life in general, daily, going about your business. As in my case it's not been a formal learning, there's not many qualifications there. As I say, it's trying to specify exactly what has been a true learning experience, as opposed to just daily living.

William might not have recognised how much learning he had actually done, 'as opposed to just daily living', had it not been for the experience of writing a CV with advice from a careers guidance worker.

William's story illustrates the complex relations between learning at and for work, and other parts of his life. In making sense of this, we can start by exploring the significance of gender and social class. We could also see William as a man of his times, a member of a particular generation who was born to working class parents at a period when the economy was dominated by manufacturing and heavy industry, came of age at a time of full employment, and lived through the deindustrialisation processes of the 1970s and 1980s. We consider generational dimensions of identity and learning more fully in Chapter 5, but we should bear in mind this linkage between personal biography and public history as we examine the issues of class and gender that have been so influential on William's position.

In many ways, William's story exemplifies a narrative of upward social mobility among working class men. This is a familiar story for readers of 1960s novels such as John Braine's *Room at the Top* or David Storey's *Saville*. His early life in a mining community was breached by his attendance at a grammar school, bringing real educational benefits along with equally important tensions and dilemmas, centred on issues of identity, loyalty and belonging. This is reinforced when he rejects office work for manufacturing, as well as by his clear and abiding preference for learning on the job, through practical experience, a preference that he shared with many working class men of his generation. Yet his time at grammar school helped awaken an interest in art and design (his best subject at school), and these were subsequently expanded considerably through his relationships with the 'bohemian' John, and his second wife. Yet although these relationships helped him feel more comfortable with, and even enjoy, a more typically middle class style of life, his musical interests led him to join brass bands that were much more strongly associated with a male working class social milieu, of the type explored vividly in the film *Brassed Off*.

The dimensions of class and gender should not be viewed in an ahistorical manner, somehow unchanging over time. Rather, William's positions and dispositions can only be understood in relation to wider changes such as the provision of grammar school places for bright working class children (especially boys) in the 1950s, the relaxing of public attitudes to divorce and unmarried coupledom, the application of new technologies to textile manufacturing and then to textile design, the relocation of the industry in the Pacific Rim, and the changing political geography of Spain in particular and Europe more generally. His workplace learning story is therefore not only a male story, or a story of upward social mobility from the working class, but also a generational story that is played out over time. Someone from a younger age group or an older one will have been through different experiences of masculinity or social mobility.

It is also clear that in William's story workplace learning is closely interwoven with learning in other parts of his life. He expressed and developed a love of art through school and throughout his career, when he combined his knowledge and understanding of art to his growing expertise in design, his capacity for adapting to technological change, his capacity for absorbing new styles in Spain, and his business acumen. Similarly with his move to Spain, chosen initially in order to follow his girlfriend (and later wife): having derived a grasp of grammar while at school, he applied this 'formal', propositional knowledge to the much more difficult matter of learning to speak colloquial Spanish and Catalan, dealing with local customers in their own language. His love of music was an entirely separate part of his life, until he found part-time work in a music shop, where he was also making good use of his business experience, language skills, technical expertise and capacity for sociability.

As with most of our cases, other people play a significant role in William's workplace learning. Two of them – John and William's second wife – pushed him in directions that he would probably not have taken otherwise; these close connections helped him to take risks, helping him negotiate his way through turning points that resulted largely from his own decisions, rather than from decisions made by others. His capacity for sociability, expressed and developed through his brass band membership as much as his working life, also helped him to sustain a wide network of contacts and clients for his textile design business. And although he had mixed feelings about not being his own master when he took the shop job in his early sixties, he was also delighted to leave behind the relative social isolation of self-employment, and clearly relishes everyday contact with customers and colleagues. He ascribes his 'self-confidence to deal with people' to his adult experiences rather than his earlier background.

Like the others in our study, William did have a few encounters with formal educational institutions as an adult. These came when he decided to seek a new role to go alongside his now struggling design business, and went to the job centre to find out what was on offer. He clearly valued the expertise of the tutors on the IT course, as well as the more personalised support that he experienced from the careers guidance workers. He also attended a course for older workers looking for a career change, which he praised for helping him realise that he could counter a lack of qualifications by identifying the skills and knowledge he had gained informally, throughout his working life. He tells of the support he received from fellow students (and which he no doubt reciprocated).

## Conclusions

In this chapter, we have drawn attention to some of the more significant aspects of informal learning in people's lives. Informal learning is a ubiquitous process that people undertake throughout their lives, including when they are taking part in a formal educational programme. Through this process of informal learning, people are sometimes reinforcing their positions and dispositions over time, sometimes altering or even transforming them, and sometimes engaging in a mixture of the two. It can, then, be understood metaphorically as a process of becoming (Hodkinson et al. 2008b).

This is not to suggest that such becoming always has a clearly defined goal. In some cases, our interviewees' stories suggest that they have a specific aim in mind when they are striving to learn. On other occasions, the learning is more or less incidental. Indeed, most informal learning is unintentional, and this has practical implications for the ways that more formal learning is organised. When attempts are made, by policy makers or educational managers, to promote particular learning processes and outcomes, there are likely to be additional unforeseen and unintended processes and outcomes, which may sometimes be more powerful than those intended. Some of these unintended consequences may have negative effects on people's attitudes towards formal learning, but sometimes they complement and support them.

Our research has also shown that informal learning is often deeply implicated in people's lives. We are not saying that it is 'embedded' in their lives, with other aspects merely serving as a backdrop or context to the learning, but rather that it is an important component of the life in which the various factors are interwoven with one another, and constantly interact with one another. Changes in relationships, work roles, leisure activities or belief systems are not simply part of the scenery, with learning centre stage; they form parts of a web of activity and meaning in which learning is deeply implicated. We therefore see attempts to record and assess informal learning as profoundly flawed. Most informal learning is 'below the surface' (Straka 2004: 14) for good reasons. The practical prospects of designing standard mechanisms for assessing this complex variety of informal learning are virtually nil.

We see all learning as capable of being understood through the four metaphors we have explored. There is certainly some virtue in understanding some learning as mainly about acquisition, though there is not much to be gained in the way of exciting insights into either the learning or the life from this metaphor. There is considerably more to be gained from understanding learning as participation and construction. Above all, though, it is best understood as a process of becoming, some of which is highly significant and some of it fairly trivial. The most trivial aspects of learning are often unnoticed, though they can often be talked about (as when you learn that your favourite football team are not as good as you hoped, which can be a weekly event for some sides). Trivial or significant, they happen nonetheless. If learning is understood in this way, as a process of becoming, then it ends only with death.

# Chapter 3

# Formal education and training

## Introduction

As we show throughout this book, learning is integral to all aspects of life. In this sense, the terms 'lifelong learning' and 'learning lives' are tautological. However, there are significant times in many people's lives when there are much more deliberate attempts to learn something specific, through the provision of taught courses, of various types. This chapter is directly concerned with what the Learning Lives research tells us about people's experiences of such courses, and the impact of attending courses on them and their lives.

A common way of distinguishing between learning on such courses and learning in other parts of a person's life is to call the former 'formal' and the latter 'informal'. As we say in Chapter 2, this apparently simple division between formal and informal learning is highly problematic. In this chapter, we use the term 'formal education and training' as shorthand for planned courses of a wide variety of types, which were attended by our research participants. We have chosen to devote a whole chapter to this because most policy and practice aimed at providing or improving learning is heavily focused on such 'formal' provision (Field 2006), and the Learning Lives data provide valuable insights that have significant implications for such policy and practice.

## Intended outcomes from formal education and training

With most of the education and training provision that we term formal, there are pre-specified intended outcomes, which are embedded in the curriculum and content of the course. Such outcomes set out, implicitly or explicitly, what a student should have learned once the course has been completed. These intended outcomes can include knowledge and understanding, skills and practical abilities, in varied combinations (Beck 2003; Gardner 2006). In addition, some formal provision is intended to give the successful student a recognised qualification, which is intended to have exchange value in educational or labour markets.

Many of our Learning Lives participants achieved these sorts of outcome from courses they attended. This could happen at different times in a person's life. In this book we concentrate upon learning in adult lives, but many of our subjects gained significant outcomes of this type from their schooling. A significant minority re-engaged in substantial periods of formal education as adults. For many, this happened in their early adult lives, whilst a smaller number returned to education when they were much older – sometimes more than once.

To answer the question about who actually participates in education or training as adults and how frequently do they do so, we conducted several analyses using the BHPS data set. The longitudinal structure of these data made it possible to map the extent of participation over time by tracking the same individuals over a fourteen-year period (1992–2005). In our analysis we took all respondents living in England who answered either 'yes' or 'no' every year to the question about whether they had participated in any part-time training schemes or courses during the preceding year. This question has been asked of all BHPS respondents since 1992. In the first wave (1991) it was only asked of those of working age, that is, women who were 16–59 and men who were 16–64. Providing an answer to this question each year for the fourteen-year observation period was a condition for entering our analytic sample. This resulted in a sample of 4,325 adults, made up of 1,922 males and 2,403 females.

Our results are summarised in Table 3.1, which show that around one quarter took at least one part-time course in 1992, falling to under one in six by 2005. This finding of course is for a longitudinal sample, and we might expect participation to fall as people become older. However, the broad pattern is consistent with the findings of Aldridge and Tuckett, based on repeated cross-sectional surveys showing a decline in the number of current learners in Britain between the late 1990s and 2005 (Aldridge and Tuckett 2007: 9). The number of BHPS respondents who said they had participated in each year is provided in column 2.

Of course, some people took courses in more than one year, while others did not take any part-time courses at all. We found that one third ($n = 1,474$, 34 per cent) reported that they had not participated at all during the entire fourteen years, leaving two thirds ($n = 2851$, 66 per cent) who reported that they had participated at least once. So if the first principal finding is that around one third of the sample are firmly lodged in the non-participant group, the second principal finding of this analysis was the insights we gained into the relatively large numbers that moved in and out of training schemes and courses frequently, moderately and less frequently. Moreover, this is quite a large proportion of those who participate. Nevertheless, only a handful ($n = 18$, 0.4 per cent) said they had participated every year over the fourteen-year period, most ($n$

= 3920, 91 per cent) said they had participated in only eight or fewer years.

This fourteen-year tracking, whilst extensive, sampled only BHPS respondents living in England. This was because the survey put the question on learning to the English sub-sample in every wave of BHPS, and was added subsequently in other UK nations. A separate analysis suggests that patterns of participation vary considerably across the four UK nations (Macleod and Lambe 2007). Using the same question and data from the seven BHPS waves 1997 to 2003, we found that fewer Welsh adults (18–21 per cent), and even fewer Scottish adults (15–18 per cent), compared to English adults (20–23 per cent), said they participated in the seven waves in which comparison between the three nations was possible. A representative sample of households in Northern Ireland joined the BHPS for the first time in 2001 making comparison possible for three consecutive waves. Utilising data from these three waves we found that only one in seven adults in Northern Ireland (14–16 per cent) said they participated compared to one in five adults in England. Again, these differences between the four home nations are consistent with the findings of cross-sectional surveys (Tuckett and Aldridge 2010).

At least since the then Prime Minister's, James Callaghan, famous speech at Ruskin College in 1976, the intended outcomes of formal education and training in the UK have been primarily focused on employment and career development. Thus, even non-vocational educational qualifications are increasingly assumed to be for a combination of educational progression and entry into the labour market. Following the election of a Labour Government in 1997, gaining employment has been seen both as a means of pursuing economic growth and competitiveness, and as the main means of increasing social inclusion. Increasingly, adult education provision has thus been seen as intended to increase students' or trainees' employability. This was one of the main policy imperatives behind pushes to improve literacy and numeracy skills, for example. In addition, much formal provision is more explicitly linked to employment, through vocational courses at college or university or through training programmes provided by employers or private training organisations.

The BHPS question on participation in part-time training schemes and courses defines formal adult learning, at least potentially, as being job related. This implies a view that education is just for the economy, and to some extent the design of the BHPS reflects this perspective. The instructions to interviewers make it clear that the question on participation was explicitly designed to exclude courses undertaken as pastime, hobby or solely for general interest but to include government training schemes, open university courses, correspondence courses and work experience schemes. It was also designed to exclude those who had participated in full-time education as full-time participation had been asked about earlier in the interview. So this BHPS question reflected policy makers' concerns for adult education to meet economic and social policy objectives, and, by implication, for learners to be of a certain type, the type that will meet widening participation and economic objectives. So in this sense our analysis of BHPS data represents an enquiry into the type of people who participate in this type of learning.

## Learning and the labour market

Generally speaking, if an adult was not part of the labour force then they were much less likely to be a participant in adult education or training as defined by the BHPS. Later in the chapter we report on some of the age, gender and class consequences this interlocking of work and educational participation trajectories had for individual learners and their access to learning. For now, we note that as well as the division between employment and non-employment, the manual/non-manual divide also had an impact on participation as did social role transitions that took young adults, and young women in particular, away from the employment market and, by implication, participation opportunities.

There are many examples of these variations in the Learning Lives data. In his early adult life, Stephen Connor worked for a TV rental company. There were frequent innovations in the electronics industry and frequent courses to enable their introduction. Stephen moved into supervisory roles fairly early on in his career, becoming responsible for organizing the work, and was always one of the first to be sent on a course. He describes the courses as essential. There was no one more experienced to learn from locally, and the skills couldn't be developed by 'working it out for yourself'. The courses were organised by the firm for whom he worked. Before the introduction of BBC 2 and colour TV he went to London for a week every month for three years. He was responsible for passing on his knowledge – acquired initially through formal learning and then through practical experience – to younger workers.

Timothy Kean had always wanted to be an actor. In middle age, whilst doing a series of casual jobs, he went to evening classes in acting. These went so well, that he changed his work to part-time and signed on for an acting course, which he has supplemented with private study in singing and languages. He was using formal training in a deliberate attempt to embark on an acting career in his middle fifties.

UK national policies tend to assume that government, providers and students all share precisely the same intentions about the outcomes of formal education and training. However, this is not always the case in practice, and our research shows many examples of people undertaking courses with intentions that differ at least in some degree from those of the government and providers. For example, Joe Price had emigrated to England from the West Indies when a boy. In adult life, he became progressively more involved in his local black West Indian community. He became aware of the prejudice against them, especially from the police in the 1970s. He saw friends 'picked on' apparently unreasonably by the police. As he became committed and started taking a more active role (for instance, by helping the younger generation), he wanted to know more and joined courses being organised in the community to increase self-pride and self-help. He attended Black History classes to improve his understanding of his own and the community's roots, and courses about the British legal system to enable him to avoid trouble and help others. His intended outcome was to know more black history, but he saw this as a means to personal, social and political ends, and it had little to do with either qualification achievement or employment as such.

Another assumption of government policy intentions for education, particularly in England, is that normally adult students should progressively climb a qualification ladder. It follows that any new qualification for learners should be at a higher level than any that they have taken before. For example, in 2007 the government instructed the Higher Education Funding Council for England (HEFCE) to withdraw funding for student on courses that led to qualifications equivalent or lower than those they had already taken (Denham 2007). However, the BHPS data clearly shows that the formal education and training that adults participate in does not always take this neatly sequenced form.

We examined patterns of movement between qualifications of different levels by people sampled in BHPS. As part of our tracking of participation patterns, trends and outcomes over time amongst the sample of 4,325 English adults, we monitored all new qualifications obtained from their part-time participation in education and training and contrasted these with the highest level of qualification a given individual had hitherto achieved (Macleod and Lambe 2008). We devised a simple classification measure so that we could distinguish between different types and levels of qualifications using the current national qualifications framework. In this way we were able to discern whether a new qualification represented progression to a higher level, or was at a similar level, or a lower level than a given individual's highest previously achieved qualification. Our findings are shown in columns 5, 6 and 7 in Table 3.1. The middle column (column 4) lists those qualifications that did not fit the current UK framework, which are likely to be 'in-house' qualifications where little is known about their portability beyond the individual's current place of work.

Table 3.1 shows first that most participation spells did not lead to a qualification of any kind. This represents the overwhelming majority of participation, particularly in the period before the election of the Labour Government. Second, most of the spells of participation that did result in a qualification led to qualifications that did not fit the current UK level of qualifications framework. Third, when qualifications had been obtained that fitted the current UK framework they were almost invariably either at the same level or a lower level than the highest qualification

*Table 3.1* Qualifications level obtained 1992–2005 relative to each respondent's previously held highest qualification

| Wave | Number participating | Total number of new qualifications | Unable to classify | Higher level | Same level | Lower level |
|------|------|------|------|------|------|------|
| 1992 | 1116 | 190 | 76 | 18 | 35 | 61 |
| 1993 | 1082 | 192 | 96 | 0 | 63 | 33 |
| 1994 | 1100 | 166 | 81 | 2 | 30 | 53 |
| 1995 | 1076 | 184 | 71 | 4 | 44 | 65 |
| 1996 | 1100 | 223 | 85 | 5 | 47 | 86 |
| 1997 | 1051 | 208 | 92 | 3 | 39 | 74 |
| 1998 | 832 | 242 | 149 | 3 | 25 | 65 |
| 1999 | 826 | 215 | 134 | 3 | 21 | 57 |
| 2000 | 930 | 239 | 163 | 2 | 16 | 58 |
| 2001 | 861 | 254 | 169 | 3 | 19 | 63 |
| 2002 | 824 | 211 | 147 | 5 | 14 | 45 |
| 2003 | 795 | 199 | 146 | 4 | 9 | 40 |
| 2004 | 783 | 226 | 146 | 1 | 16 | 63 |
| 2005 | 709 | 245 | 151 | 3 | 13 | 78 |

that that individual had hitherto obtained. In fact, only in one respect did we find a pattern that conformed to government intentions: over time, although the number of participants fell, there was a sharp rise in the number of qualifications gained; even so, as we have seen, most of these qualifications fell outside the national qualifications framework. The trajectory of engagement and re-engagement for most people seems, then, to follow complex and highly differentiated patterns, rather than falling neatly into a tidy administrative sequence. Our qualitative data show that this can often be understood through people's motives for engaging and re-engaging.

## Education, training and personal, social growth and change

Joe Price's story shows that even when a student or trainee explicitly wishes to achieve some of the intended outcomes of a course, there are often wider more personal reasons for participating. Some adults in our research re-engaged with formal education and training during periods of significant personal change. Such major personal turning points (Strauss 1962) often involved changes in several aspects of a person's life. Triggers included changes such as divorce, bereavement, retirement, redundancy, migration, illness, or simply a desire to change the way of life. Though many people make such changes without formal education and training, our research suggests that it is during these times of change that adults are more likely to re-engage. Sometimes problems with employment form an important strand in such turning points.

Later in his life, Joe Price became bankrupt, triggering a serious personal crisis. He was placed on the New Deal programme for the long-term unemployed. This made him identify a possible new career in computers. He was sent on college courses to develop employment skills. He found the courses interesting and started upgrading and reselling old computers from home, for other students. During his next computer course, he was spotted by a tutor who knew him from his time in the electrical industry. This tutor persuaded him to teach computing, and Joe found that he enjoyed teaching and was successful. The college sent him on a part-time course to obtain a teaching qualification. This led in turn to his enrolment for a foundation degree in education. However, whilst further education and training played an important role for Joe, he is clear that it was finding religion that was the main means of overcoming his personal crisis and changing his life.

Wafa Jabeen's story is an example of the role of formal education within a personal turning point that is not centrally concerned with employment. Wafa is of Pakistani descent and a Muslim. She had studied for a BEd and worked as a teacher. She and her husband had lived in London in their own flat. Wafa enjoyed work as a primary teacher and life in London with theatres and cinemas. However, after five years, 'I became pregnant and we both thought it best to move back [to a northern city], because we had family over here, and there our lives weren't suited ... to bring up a child.'

Wafa moved in with her husband's extended family. She described the following six months, during which her husband remained in London to sell their flat, as the worst experience of her life. Instead of receiving the family support she had expected, her experience was a very unhappy one:

> There was a lot of family politics going on, that I wasn't aware of, because I've never come across it before... At first I couldn't understand why people were behaving as they were, towards me. I found a lot of their behaviour very hurtful... She [mother-in-law] treated me very badly, and his brother and sisters, now, thinking about it, I know why it was, it was all a sort of a control thing. It happens a lot in Asian families, especially extended Asian families. Especially those where the people have come over from Pakistan... When ... my son was born ... they actually started picking on *him*. And that *really* hurt me ... and I couldn't understand why they were doing it... And it wasn't just one person, they were all sort of like ganged up.

As soon as the London flat was sold Wafa and her husband bought their own house and she could escape. She felt that the 'bullying' of herself and her son had continued but she minimised contact with her in-laws. She had decided to stay at home and look after her son, and came to value the freedom from work commitments. An important part of this new life was attendance at a series of formal courses including Islamic studies. These were a way of keeping her mind active and of continuing with her earlier love of education. They fitted in well with her family routines, including taking her son to and from school. She found solace in reading the Koran where she liked what she saw there about honesty, peace and reconciliation, in contrast to some of what she saw around her.

Several older people in our sample re-engaged in formal education and training after they had finished in full-time employment. Hodkinson et al. (2008b) argued that retirement itself is a learning process that lasts several years and, for some people, formal courses play a significant part in that. William Moore, for example, went on a short course about CV writing and job applications, at a time when his lace designing business was in serious decline. He says that this course proved valuable in helping him see himself differently, and get a part-time job working in a specialist sheet music shop. This new job drew upon both his business experience and also upon his lifelong hobby as an amateur musician. Both Stephen Connor and Jim Huzzar turned to adult education to help deal with issues of boredom and associated stress, even depression, during early retirement. For them, like many others, it was the process of participating in education that was valuable, rather than learning prescribed content and achieving the officially intended outcomes of the courses they took.

Gladys Dean was in her mid-sixties when her daughter finally persuaded her to enrol in an adult literacy course. Despite successfully bringing up her children and working full-time for many years, Gladys had never learned to read and write. Hers is an excellent example of a common overlap between intended course outcomes and personal growth and change. She did indeed learn slowly to read and write, but this and the process of attending the course and participating with the tutor and other students, contributed to a major change in Gladys herself and in her life. She became both more confident and more independent, and said: 'The best life I have is now... I really love going to school [adult education classes]. What I'm learning now is for me, you know.'

## Degrees of involvement in formal education and training

Regardless of the type of course, our research shows that people engage with formal education and training in very different ways. This can be understood as a continuum between no or very low involvement and very high involvement. With no or very low involvement we mean turning up to the course with no personal commitment to it. This sometimes happened, for example, when people were sent to a compulsory training event but remained antagonistic to the course and engaged very little with what went on there. At the other end of the continuum were people with a very high level of personal involvement in education, so that participating in courses became a very important aspect of their lives, and even a significant part of their identity. Between these two extremes lies a wide range of variations.

Lower levels of involvement in formal education and training can be beneficial, if the main purpose of that involvement is simply to achieve some of the explicitly intended outcomes of the course. We have already seen how William Moore gained a lot from a short course on job applications and CV writing. Colin Farmer had spent many years working as a house husband. He wanted to get a job to take some of the pressure of earning off his wife, but lacked confidence or knowledge about how to do this. A careers adviser suggested a computer course and a course in volunteering, which he dutifully completed with misgivings about the point of it all. But besides the actual skills he learned, the courses gave him some insights into what had been going on in the world of employment since he left it fifteen years earlier. Each was followed by further months of indecision and loss of confidence. So it was a particular pleasure when he was offered the first job he did apply for. He was to be the art and technology technician at a local secondary school, using many of his previously informally learned skills.

The research also showed examples where low levels of involvement and forced attendance had more negative effects. Billy Milroy trained as a chef, but while he still enjoys cooking – mainly for his family – he does not wish to work the long hours in catering. Currently out of work, he has attended access courses designed to bridge gaps between long-term unemployment and education or employment. Earlier on, he had also been required to undergo retraining during a previous spell of unemployment, describing these compulsory courses as 'pretty shit'. Certainly there was no sign that the compulsory courses had stimulated him or influenced his ability to shape his own life in any way.

Kathleen Donnelly, in her mid-thirties by time of our last interview, and 'at a crossroads' in her life, worked for the post office after leaving school. She hated this job and occupied her time with a fast-paced social life of drink, dance and drugs, leading what she calls her 'magazine lifestyle'. After becoming a single parent, she had taken a Higher National Diploma in social science, combining a rather weakly formulated hope for educational progression with the aim of getting out of the house and meeting people. She was then advised to pursue a Scottish Vocational Qualification (SVQ) course in community development with a view to finding a professional role as a youth worker, but in the event it resulted in cynicism. She felt manipulated by the SVQ system, which, she believes, allows professionals working in community development to advance their own interests.

> It's just been another government run scheme where they're just, I've seen that many people just using poor people to make a profit, they're making profit out of poverty and it's annoying me because when we

started on this project it was all full of this great ethos where 'You'll go out and do good for the community, it's people like you that are needed, you'll get a qualification, we've got 100 per cent success rate in jobs and stuff.' I have wrote sixteen or seventeen job applications and CVs out and not one company has said 'Sorry you've been unsuccessful', not one of them and I think it's a bunch of lies, I think the whole thing's a bunch of lies, but I don't know how to protest about it.

Working for the qualification itself, she said, was just 'ticking boxes'. She felt 'cheated, really cheated' and was uncertain about her future. Rather than deepening her involvement in learning, she was far less involved than she had been before starting the SVQ.

High levels of involvement in formal education and training sometimes occurred for a significant period in a person's life. Stephen Connor was highly involved in his regular TV training courses, gaining much enjoyment and personal satisfaction from the role they played in his leading troubleshooter role at work. For Jim Huzzar there was a period of sustained high involvement after he had retired. Jim Huzzar went back to formal education to deal with boredom and depression in retirement.

[Someone] told me about this place [local adult education centre], so I thought fair enough I'll come, so I booked for maths and computers and I've got myself an old computer that I messed about with at home and I found I really enjoyed doing it and the maths. Me basic maths were OK but I've never done algebra in me life, we never did anything like that at school... So I thought I'd have a go. I've been coming about five years now and I've been lucky enough that I've gone in for exams I've got through most of 'em, which is fair enough and I've got to admit I feel a bit chuffed myself.

He had recently undertaken a creative writing course. 'I've always been a reader, and they said, "Would you like to try this creative writing class?" ... I've never written owt in me life apart from betting slips.' He tried it, and developed a good relationship with the tutor, who not only provided interesting ideas for them to write about but allowed Jim to go off and write whatever he wanted when he felt inspired: 'I really enjoyed it, and I've got to admit I like coming down here, I like the people, I like the tutors, there's nothing I can say that I dislike.'

At the time of the research he was doing five courses a week, and his wife did a different one. They had various separate activities sorted out through the week, and Jim felt that their relationship was the better for it. Jim had progressed as far as he could with the maths locally, but didn't want to go elsewhere to reach a higher level. He wanted to stay at this local centre where he knew people. He had completed and passed several exams but didn't know what they all were. He was happy to do the exams and get certificates but not really bothered. 'I'm not worried about going in for exams but obviously the lass [tutor] has a job to do so if nobody went in for exams they'd say, "What the hell is she doing here?"' He also didn't enter if he thought he might fail: 'If I fail I feel as if I've let the girl down.' To Jim, the success of these courses was in keeping his mind active, engaging in interesting activities, learning new and interesting things and having a social life outside the family. Thus being a student had become a significant part of his identity.

For a small but significant number of people, high levels of involvement in formal learning continue for very long periods throughout their lives. We interviewed three people well past formal retirement age, for whom education had always been important. All were women. Our repeated cross-sectional analysis of the BHPS shows that more females than males said they had participated in part-time education and training. This was also our finding when we changed our definition of participation to include only those courses that were designed to lead to a qualification and to include both full- and part-time attendance. We found that in the full sub-sample of BHPS respondents aged 25–64 living in Wales women were one and a half times more likely to participate than men. Also when we considered gender in relation to place of learning we found a marked difference in the proportions of females and males attending educational institutions, with a trend that stays within the 60–70 per cent margin over time for females compared to a margin of 30–40 per cent for males. It would seem then that women are more likely to learn in public institutions in their own time. We found some interlocking of class and gender preferences as the bulk of these women attending educational institutions were middle class. We also found that almost half of women's participation in employment-based provision was among the professional and managerial occupations, compared to only one in five women in routine services industries (education, medicine, care, hospitality, etc.) and intermediate occupations (clerical, administrative, sales, technical, service, etc.).

Although to some extent these findings indicate a trend in favour of women, and middle class women in particular, when we followed the same individuals across time we found a more nuanced picture as we uncovered some gender effects that had remained hidden in cross-sectional analyses. This was most evident amongst the younger cohorts studied (1997 school leavers and those born between 1966 and 1971) where young women were significantly less likely than young men to participate. We return to this issue later in the chapter.

Jennifer Whitefield had pursued formal learning all her life. She was successful at school but left in rebellious mode before completing her A levels. After a short period of unemployment she joined the army. They provided training for all the jobs they needed undertaken but also encouraged and financed personal learning. As soon as she was established in an office job that was well within her capacity, Jennifer revived her interest in learning languages, gaining several A and O levels through correspondence courses. She'd have liked to go to university to study linguistics when she came out of the army but her A levels weren't good enough. So she did a degree equivalent college diploma in business and languages, passing in addition professional exams in translation. Boyfriend and marriage made a move into a translation career difficult so she went on to train as a further education (FE) teacher. By the end of the research she was in her late fifties, and was working as a translator. Throughout her working life she took courses to enhance her careers and for personal interest.

Jennifer's moderately high levels of involvement in formal education and training were reinforced by her frequent successes in achieving the intended outcomes of those courses: finishing and achieving the relevant qualifications. For her, however, this was part of something wider – her enjoyment of being a student and of attending courses, and the way in which going on courses was a frequent and important part of her life. However, for Jennifer education was always part of something bigger – her wider life. The same was true for Jane Eddington, who also went on many formal courses throughout her life to date. However, Jane's story is different from that of Jennifer, in important respects.

For Jane, many of her forays into formal education resulted in failure, from the official, intended outcomes perspective. For a series of reasons she did not always complete courses, and consequently did not always achieve the intended qualification. Despite this, she felt she had learned a lot from the courses she went on, and persisted, from time to time, in going on others. For Jane, learning from such courses was an integral part of a much wider learning agenda. She was both knowledgeable and enthusiastic about Mediterranean history and culture, learning from visits, reading, museums and the internet, as well as formal courses. Some of the formal courses she went on were linked to this pervasive interest, which partly began in an A level course taken when still at school. Other courses had more instrumental purposes, including being directed, by the local Job Centre, to a course that trained volunteers to provide advocacy support for people with disabilities. Our research suggests that being a learner, including attending formal courses, was a key part of Jane's self-identity. Her involvement in most formal courses was uniformly high, despite the fact that she did not always complete them.

## The relationships between informal learning and learning on formal courses

We have already mentioned some of the problems with classifying learning as either formal or informal. In fact, in almost all cases, where learning on a formal course was seen as valuable by the learner, there were strong links with informal learning elsewhere in their lives. In this sense, Jane Eddington's story is illustrative of a more general point. Stephen Connor's

TV training was valuable because he fully integrated it into his working practices. Jim Huzzar's adult education classes were valuable as part of his life and personal growth, which included much informal learning as well. Joe Price used his black history to aid his activism on behalf of his neighbours and compatriots. William Moore found learning about job applications helpful, in relation to much informal learning he had engaged in before, during and after changing jobs. For Gladys Dean, the formally acquired literacy skills were reinforced by using those skills in everyday life, and the value of the course to her lay in its catalyst effect in changing her life. That changing life resulted in further informal learning, without which the course itself would have had much less impact. This interrelationship between formal and informal learning can also be clearly seen in our final example of someone with high involvement in formal education.

Anna Reynard was nearly 70 when fieldwork finished. She said, more than once, that, 'I've always felt that education was the leitmotif in my life.' She had always had a passion for learning – which she perceived more broadly than formal education. This encompassed a passion for learning for herself and a desire to share that passion with others; in particular with those from disadvantaged backgrounds who have not had the same opportunities to enjoy learning.

Anna was successful at school and then studied languages at university. She wanted to write after graduating, but was talked into getting a teaching qualification. After her first teaching job, Anna had a five-year career break bringing up her children. During this time she read a lot. She took a short Preschool Playgroups Association course before running a playgroup in a neighbouring estate, and a children's library group. She did a Post-graduate Diploma in Educational Psychology and Sociology, but didn't complete the dissertation to turn it into a Master's degree, because she started looking for a job again.

When her boys had started school she went back to teaching in a local council estate primary school, which she found rewarding, but the job was only temporary. Unable to find another similar job, she applied for a teacher training post at a higher education (HE) institution. This was again temporary, part of a succession of part-time and fixed-term jobs. The one that best suited her self-view was as a field officer setting up and evaluating projects in an initiative to improve the educational opportunities of disadvantaged groups. When that was shut down by the government, similar jobs were only available at a distance, which she saw as too great a risk to her family life, so she took a post locally as an educational social worker. She liked being able to work directly with families with problems, but after four years the system required her to take a social work qualification. This was one course she didn't want to do as it would have moved her away from her educational focus and duplicated what her husband was by now doing. She tried doing some freelance educational writing, then worked at an FE college teaching 'pre-social work' students. Then the HE college offered her a series of short contracts back in teacher training. She enjoyed the work, but became frustrated as she was not eligible for promotion or training. The requirement then was that teacher trainers should update their own skills through 'recent and relevant' school experience. She believed this was right and that it should apply to her.

Although enthusiastic about doing courses, Anna believed strongly in learning through experience and practice and in many other less formal ways. This perceived need to learn from up-to-date practical experience in a school classroom led her to leave teacher training and return to schools. She deliberately applied to a school in a poorer area. She had high ideals on teaching methods to inspire all, but these did not help her to deal with the difficult classes, nor did she have any support from her head of department. Her temporary contract was not renewed. Through school networks she learned of a job in a similarly deprived area but where there was a strong ethos of support for staff and pupils and belief that the system could work. She took the job even though it involved long journeys every day. Although there was support and the school's ethos fitted her own, she still struggled with many of the classes, and after a few years, coming close to a nervous breakdown and crisis of identity, she decided that the long journey was too much. She took a job in a 'nicer' area nearer home. Some classes were still problematic and she thinks now that there may have been a failure to learn on her part – perhaps too determined an adherence to ideals. She was happy to leave school teaching when she won a bursary at her old HE college to study for a PhD.

She completed her PhD and published a book based on it, and then her husband of 35 years died. Since then she has had no further paid employment, but has become deeply involved with the University of the Third Age (U3A), as organiser, volunteer teacher and student. She leads an active life pursuing this and other hobbies and interests. Her activities have provided the social networks where she has found new partners. At the time of her first interview she expressed envy of the researcher's position and would clearly have liked a job in educational research. However, having spent the next three years enjoying a life where she could pursue interests, visit relatives and friends, and take holidays when she wanted, by her final interview she was no longer interested in taking on any serious long-term commitments that would restrict her flexibility.

She was still happy with her commitment to U3A, and liked the fact that its short teaching terms provide a framework for her life. It remained important to her that she should still be doing things that help other people. However, she said she recognises that it is time to pull back a bit and not get involved in major emotional battles where things are not going how she would like them to. The deaths of people she was close to have, she thinks, made her aware of her own mortality and the need to get on with things she wants to do for herself. She is also trying to take greater care of her own health. Over the whole period she has attended exercise classes and dancing classes in term time, and organised a walking group.

## Access to formal education and training

The Learning Lives research shows that adult access to and involvement in formal education and training are very uneven. When all BHPS respondents 1997–2004 who answered 'yes' to the initial question on participation were asked where the main place of learning was, most answered that it was employment based and that the learning was provided by their employers (40 per cent + over time). In contrast, those who said their learning took place at an employment centre or employment club, which are places mainly geared towards helping the unemployed find work, barely registered (less than 1 per cent over time). These findings were observed when the UK data were aggregated and little variation to this trend was observed at each of the four home nation levels. A reasonable inference is that most of the part-time learning as measured by the BHPS takes place in working hours and is provided and paid for by employers. If this is the case then it may also be that training opportunities are made available to some but not others as employers act as providers and gatekeepers.

The evidence would appear to support this potentially negative consequence of the interconnectedness of (un)employment and (non-) participation. Age emerged as a powerful indictor of participation with virtually no one participating from age 54 onwards. This was particularly evident in our longitudinal analysis, which followed the same individuals across time and strongly suggested that the older age groups just stop participating around their mid-fifties. It seems then that as far as vocational training is concerned, which was largely what our question was measuring, older people who are highly likely to be either out of the workforce or moving out of the workforce, are all but excluded. On the other hand, young men and women whom we characterised using various criteria as being 'work-oriented' were the most likely group to participate. But gender differences emerged as they moved into their late twenties and thirties. Whilst marital transitions decreased the likelihood of participation amongst both males and females, parenthood transitions had a far greater effect on decreasing the likelihood of female participation and increased, though less markedly, the likelihood of male participation. For many of these young women we found that parenthood transitions coincided with movement out of the workforce.

Gender differences did not always favour women. Young male participation levels were higher than those for most other groups, a feature we observed when we tracked 463 BHPS respondents from across Britain who had left continuous full-time schooling in 1997 over a six-year period until 2004. We found that young males were significantly more likely to return to formal adult learning than young females and that this difference persisted over time. But this difference did not kick in until two years after leaving full-time schooling. In other words, if a female leaver had not returned to adult learning within two years of leaving full-time education then she was significantly (84 per cent) less likely to return than her male counterpart.

Gender thus emerged as an important predictor of becoming a participant in formal learning amongst young school leavers. Further analysis revealed that this might be connected to increased domestic responsibilities in the form of marriage/cohabitation and parenthood transitions, which had a greater likelihood of decreasing participation amongst young women than amongst young men. Alongside these findings we observed a clear link between unemployment and participation with the estimated odds of those whose status was recorded as unemployed at the beginning of the observation period participating in formal learning were 54 per cent of those whose status was recorded as employed at the same time point. We further found that a social role transition from employment to unemployment during the observation period reduced the odds of participating by 50 per cent compared to those who had not experienced this role status change.

But there was evidence that younger women were finding new ways of accessing learning or delaying learning despite being separated from work and job-related training through possibly the impact of social role change. We found a steep upturn in the take-up of home-based learning amongst women, particularly in the period 1998–2001. Also women who had made an early transition into parenthood had a higher probability than their male and female counterparts of returning to formal learning later on.

Social class differences emerged as a strong predictor of non-participation in our characterisation of the sub-group of the adult population that persistently failed to participate over time. This analysis revealed that non-participants over our fourteen-year observation period (1992–2005) were highly likely to have left school at the first opportunity, to have a parent in a manual occupation when they were age fourteen, and to have a father and mother who had left school with no qualifications. We found a strong relationship between prior learning and, separately, employment, including the nature of that employment in terms of the manual/non-manual divide, and the odds of being a frequent participant. Non-manual workers were twice as likely as manual workers to be participants when we examined seven waves of data from 1997–2003, with remarkably little variance in these ratios over time or between the four home nations.

Likewise social class emerged as a key indicator of participation in our tracking of 1997 school leavers. We found that (1) the estimated odds of those who had left initial phase education with no or low qualifications becoming a participant were 51 per cent of those who had left with higher level qualifications; (2) the estimated odds of those whose household per capita income was recorded as being in the lowest quintile at the beginning of the observation period participating were 74 per cent of those whose household per capita income was not in the bottom quintile at the same time point; and (3) the estimated odds of those whose household tenure at the beginning of the observation period was recorded as 'non-owner–occupier' participating was 70 per cent of those whose household tenure was recorded as owner–occupier at the same time point.

## The impact of formal education and training on a person's dispositions

When adults think about or engage in formal education and training, they do so with already established personal and social dispositions. By dispositions we mean deeply held orientations towards life, which are often at least partly tacit (we discuss this idea further in Chapter 6). Gladys Dean was embarrassed about her lack of literacy, and frightened of going back to what she called 'school'. Anna Reynard was deeply committed to both education and working for a more equal society, and approached all of her many courses from this perspective. These deeply held dispositions sometimes contributed to either the success or failure of the formal learning engagement. Tony Wilf, for example, had a very negative experience of secondary schooling. When he enrolled in adult education classes as an older man, these dispositions affected the ways in which he responded to classes and especially tutors. When one tutor of English acted in ways that reminded Tony of his school teachers, he rapidly abandoned the course. When other tutors acted differently and treated him in ways he was comfortable with, he continued and progressed. When Stephen Connor did his TV training, he went on the courses already positively disposed towards them, because of the benefits they brought to him in his job.

Once on a course, participation can influence a person's prior dispositions in a variety of ways. Where there is low or no involvement, there may be little or no impact. Where the levels of involvement are moderate or high, participation in formal education and training can sometimes reinforce existing dispositions, and sometimes contribute to changing them. Because people hold many different, overlapping and sometimes contradictory dispositions, it is not unusual for both reinforcement and change to happen at the same time.

In Wafa Jabeen's case, the courses she took whilst a mother of a young child helped reinforce her dispositions both with respect of her love of intellectual stimulation, and her decision not to work full-time whilst her child was at school. More subtly, the course in Muslim studies helped her retain her own strong religious faith, whilst rejecting the ways in which she had been treated by her in-laws. For Stephen Connor, the TV training courses simply reinforced his dispositions and identity as an expert and troubleshooter, within the rental firm for which he worked. For Joe Price, the computing and teaching courses he took helped him develop a different career, contributing, with his religious conversion, to major dispositional and identity changes. Jim Huzzar's dispositions and self-identity were significantly changed by his ongoing high-level involvement in a series of adult education courses at his local centre. Tony Wilf had a similar experience, but he was only prepared to change so far. Tony was determined that education would not make him 'posh, like my brother'. Put differently, he worked hard not to let course attendance change his strong male working class identity.

Our research also shows that the impact of formal education and training upon a person's dispositions and identity are determined by far more than just the nature of the course itself. However, there are suggestions that very short courses with lower levels of involvement are often less effective than longer courses with higher levels of involvement in bringing about significant personal change. Short courses can help bring about such change in two circumstances. First, if short courses are parts of what to the person is a longer period of engagement with formal education and training, they may contribute to something bigger than each course seen in isolation. Second, a short course may make a difference is it acts as a catalyst in a much bigger change scenario. This happened when William Moore took a very short course in job applications and CV writing.

## Conclusions

Issues of course length, levels of involvement and personal change are important for those planning and providing adult education provision. We conclude, therefore, with a summary of some of the main implications of this chapter for the planning and provision of adult education.

- Very short courses, often used by employers and increasingly popular in government-funded adult education in England, can be effective in helping people learn very specific content, but are unlikely to lead to personal change, unless part of something much bigger.
- Adults vary considerably in their levels of involvement with courses they attend. Higher levels of involvement are more likely to result in personal growth and development.
- Attending formal education and training can reinforce existing personal dispositions, or contribute to personal change.
- Personal growth and change is rarely linear, and adults often benefit from attending courses that are not explicitly aimed at a higher qualification than they have already achieved.
- Adults can benefit from formal education and training at many different times throughout their lives. Such courses may have an increased relevance at times of personal crisis and change.

- Formal education and training can be beneficial for career progression and employment, but many adults gain significant and lasting benefit from courses in relation to other aspects of their lives.
- Some groups of people, for example the poor, those living in deprived neighbourhoods, the unemployed and some retired people, have limited access to formal education and training.

# Chapter 4

# Narrative learning

## Introduction

We started the Learning Lives project with a wide and open definition of learning in order to be able to capture as many possible forms and dimensions of learning. We were first and foremost interested in what people had to say about their lives and about the role of learning in it, both retrospectively and during the three years of the data-collection period. Not surprisingly, when we asked participants in a more direct manner about their learning, almost all of them spoke about their formal education. Nonetheless many of the stories they told provided evidence that they had not only learned from their formal education but also from many of the events in their lives. Over time we became increasingly interested in the question of how people learn from their lives and in the significance of this learning for their lives. Our interest was prompted by the fact that upon reading and analysing the life stories of participants we found that in a significant number of cases the stories revealed that participants had reached some kind of insight or understanding about their lives, about themselves and about their position in the world. The stories evidenced, in other words, that the participants had learned something from their lives. We also found that such learning had an impact on the ways in which participants led their lives. We became particularly interested in the role of stories and storying in such learning processes and in the possible relationships between the characteristics of the stories themselves and the potential of narrative and narration for learning and action. Our investigations into the role of narrative and narration in learning from life led us to the development of the idea of *narrative learning* (Goodson 2006) and the subsequent development of a theory of narrative learning (Biesta et al. 2008; Tedder and Biesta 2009a, 2009b; Goodson et al. 2010). In this chapter we present our approach and give an overview of the insights we generated through our analysis. A much more detailed account can be found in Goodson et al. (2010).

## Life, story, narrative and learning

The focus of this chapter is on the stories people tell about their lives and about themselves. Such stories are not entirely optional. It is not that we can simply choose to have or not to have them. In a very fundamental sense we exist and live our lives 'in' and 'through' stories. Stories have the potential to provide our lives with continuity and endurance. They can give our lives structure, coherence and meaning, or they can provide the backdrop against which we experience our lives as complex, fragmented or without meaning. Stories do not just provide us with a *sense* of who we are. To a large extent the stories about our lives and ourselves *are* who we are.

The stories we tell about our lives can play an important role in the ways in which we learn from our lives. The relationship between life, self, story and learning is, however, a complicated one. It is not that the story is just a description of life and self, a kind of picture we can look at in order to learn from it. In a very real sense the story *constitutes* the life and the self. Life and self are thus at the same time 'object' and 'outcome' of the story. What complicates the matter further is that the self is also the author of the story. All this means that the *construction* of the story – the story*ing* of the life and the self – is a central element of the way in which we can learn from our lives through storying. We refer to this kind of learning as *narrative learning*. Narrative learning is not simply learning *from* the stories we tell about our lives and our selves but is the learning that happens *in and through* the narration.

Since storying is an integral part of how we lead our lives, narrative learning is not necessarily or exclusively a conscious process. Moreover, because stories tend to serve a communicative purpose, narrative learning is often a kind of by-product of our ongoing actions, interactions and conversations. It is only in more exceptional circumstances that we engage deliberately in narrative construction in order to learn from it. This can happen, for example, in adult education programmes that focus on autobiographical work (for example Van Houten 1998; Dominicé 2000; Rossiter and Clark 2007), and can also play a role in forms of psychotherapy. In our research, however, we were primarily interested in narrative learning as it occurs more or less spontaneously, that is, in and through the stories people tell about their lives without a particular intention to learn from such storying.

An important distinction for our discussion is that between story and narrative. With Polkinghorne (1988; see also Ricoeur 1991) we see narratives as stories with a *plot*. A plot serves as 'a type of conceptual scheme by which a contextual meaning of individual events can be displayed' (Polkinghorne 1995: 7). Narratives can thus be understood as stories with an organising principle by which the contextual meaning of individual events can be displayed and articulated. The 'emplotment' (Ricoeur) of life events most often occurs in a chronological way – depicting the life as a series of interlocking events – although emplotment can also operate in a more thematic manner.

While life narratives are subjective, they are not completely idiosyncratic. Not only do they often display the more formal characteristics of narratives, such as the presence of an actor, action, a goal, a scene and an instrument (Kenneth Burke's so-called 'pentad'; see Burke 1945), life narratives often also make use of particular 'scripts', 'archetypes' and 'genres', both with regard to the construction of the story and the construction of the self 'in' and 'through' the story. In this regard Czarniawska (2004: 5) has made the important observation that the life story (as biography and autobiography) is itself a *genre*; a genre, moreover, with a particular and recent history (the word biography became a recognised term after 1680 while the word 'autobiography' was found in English texts only in 1809). According to Bruner the 'power' of the life narrative does not depend upon its factual truth. In this respect life narratives are 'factually indifferent' (Bruner 1990: 44). This is not to say that facts do not matter, but what it does suggest is that what matters in narratives is not simply whether they correspond to reality or not, but how they *function*, both for narrators themselves and in relation to the social settings in which lives are narrated (including interview and research settings).

## A framework for analysing life stories

In analysing the stories we collected in the Learning Lives project we were particularly interested in the role stories and storying might play in how people learn from their lives. By this we were not wanting to suggest that people ought to have stories, and even less that they ought to learn from their lives and ought to do so by using stories. We have clear evidence that people can live good, happy and rewarding lives without learning, without stories and without narrative learning. We might therefore compare the stories people tell about their lives to tools – tools people can use to learn from their lives. The focus of our analysis can thus be said to be on the qualities and characteristics of these tools as we aim to understand the relationship between the narrative quality of life stories and their potential to generate learning and facilitate action. While it is also interesting to ask *why* different individuals tell different kinds of stories and do different things with them, and while there are important sociological questions to be asked about the different ways in which individuals engage with stories, narrative and learning, these questions are beyond the scope of our research, first and foremost because we approached the data generated in the Learning Lives project as narrative data, not as psychological or sociological data.

In our analysis we focused on two aspects: the *narrative quality* of life stories and storying and the *efficacy* of narrative and narration. Within the latter we made a distinction between the *learning potential* – the ways in which and the extent to which certain narratives allow for learning – and the *action potential* – the ways in which and the extent to which such learning 'translates' into action. *Narrative quality* has to do with formal characteristics of the stories people tell about their lives. We identified five dimensions that we considered important for characterising significant dimensions and differences. The first three became central to our analysis across cases; the last two highlight aspects that were relevant in relation to some but not all cases.

The first dimension of the narrative quality of life stories and storying is *narrative intensity*. This not only has to do with the length of the account and the number of words used, but also, and more importantly, with the amount of detail and the 'depth' of the account offered. We characterise narrative intensity in terms of *more or less elaborate*. The second dimension of narrative quality concerns the question of whether a story is predominantly *descriptive* or veers more towards *analysis and evaluation*. The question here is whether a story is predominantly an attempt to describe the life, or whether the story can be seen as an attempt to interpret, make sense and/or evaluate (aspects of) the life. To make sense of one's life – or, to be more precise, to construct a story that presents the life as making sense – is related to the ideas of *plot* and *emplotment*, which have to do with the presence of one or more organising principles within the life story. Although we found some cases where the life story was constructed around a clear plot, more often did we find traces of emplotment, that is, traces of organising and structuring principles within the life narrative. Plot and emplotment are important because they can be

## Analytical categories

### Five dimensions of narrative quality

1 Narrative intensity: more or less elaborate
2 Descriptive–analytical–evaluative
3 Plot/emplotment
4 Chronological–thematic
5 Theorised–vernacular

### Efficacy

1 *Learning potential*: the ways in which and the extent to which certain narratives allow for learning.
2 *Action potential*: the ways in which and the extent to which such learning 'translates' into action.

taken as evidence that the narrator has come to some kind of understanding of the life, which, in turn, can be taken as evidence of learning – albeit that narrators are not always fully aware of this themselves. In some cases life stories were clearly constructed around key insights and understandings. In other cases we were able to identify underlying themes and structuring principles within the narrative, but we were not always sure whether these also played a role in the perception of the narrators. The fourth dimension of narrative quality concerns the question whether the life is recounted in a *chronological* or a *thematic* way. Although this is a relevant distinction, we found very few non-chronological accounts. We take this as an indication that the most prevalent 'genre' of the life story, at least in the modern Western mindset, is that of a chronological account (see also Czarniawska 2004: 5). The fifth dimension of narrative quality has to do with the extent to which the narrative is in some way or form *theorised*, that is, whether the narrator presents us with a theory of life and/or self, or whether the narration veers more towards a *vernacular* account, staying more closely to everyday articulations and understandings.

The question of the *efficacy* of life stories has to do with what people can do and actually do in and through their stories and storying. A crucial distinction in this regard is that between the *learning potential* of narrative and narration and the *action potential* of narrative and narration. Learning potential refers to the ways in which and the extent to which people are able to learn from their stories and storying. The action potential has to do with the ways in which and the extent to which such learning 'translates' into action. The notion of learning potential is central to the idea of narrative learning, as it refers to the ways in which and the extent to which the life narrative and the narration of life function as 'sites' for learning.

## Case studies

Perhaps the most significant finding emerging from this part of our research is that differences in the narrative quality of the stories people tell about their lives do matter for the ways in which and the extent to which people can learn from such stories and such storying and also for the ways in which such narrative learning has consequences for people's actions. Not surprisingly, there are no one-to-one correlations between narrative quality, learning and action. But the patterns and connections that can be discerned are nonetheless interesting and noteworthy and, to the extent to which narrative learning is seen as a worthwhile and desirable form of learning, also have important practical implications. In this section we present our main findings through a discussion of the eight cases studies we discussed in much more detail in Goodson et al. (2010). These cases in themselves only represent a small selection of the much larger group of individuals involved in the Learning Lives project. Nonetheless, focusing in detail on their stories and storying helped us to generate important insights and develop our understanding of learning from life through narrative and narration. For reasons of space our accounts in this section will have to be brief and focused on the findings rather than the often intriguing detail of the cases.

While it might be tempting to focus on those individuals who have rich and detailed stories to tell about their lives, and while we initially started from the assumption that those would be the most interesting cases for our research, we learned in a sense more about the role of narrative and narration from those cases that were on the other end of the spectrum as these helped us to adjust and reconsider some of our initial expectations. Two important lessons we learned is that narratives with low narrative intensity and which are more on the descriptive and vernacular side of the spectrum are not in themselves without efficacy. We also learned that high narrative intensity, much analysis and strong emplotment are not in themselves a guarantee for efficacy as not all such narratives translate into learning, nor does all narrative learning translate into action.

### John Peel

The story of John Peel, who was born in 1927 in a small hamlet in the south-east of England as the first son and second child of a farmer and who also became a farmer himself, provided us with an example of a narrative with relatively low intensity, at least compared to others in our group. Initially John spoke for about ten minutes before declaring he was 'stuck' and asking for the recording to stop. In the intervening pause he spoke of his difficulty in telling his life story, partly because of the presence of a recorder, but also because of the 'false' conversation in trying to create a chronological account of one's life to a stranger ('chronological' being John's interpretation of the task). He later went on to complete the narration of his life, but it remained somewhat stunted and descriptive in character. John's story veered toward the descriptive end of the spectrum with some moments of analysis and reflection. Central in the story was John's identity as a farmer, which served as the organising principle around which the story was constructed. But less than to think of this as a principle through which John was trying to make sense of his life – in the sense in which this identity might have served as a plot – the farmer identity to a large extent was what John's life had been about and what John had been about. Throughout his story it was clear that John wanted to stay true to his life as a farmer and to his sense of self as a farmer. In this regard the farmer identity functioned as the 'script' of John's life story. This is not to suggest that there was no passion for the particular script of John's life or that it was without intrinsic motivation. On the contrary, there was strong personal involvement. Farming was embodied in John and his story speaks strongly to this. While there was evidence of learning in John's life, we did not get the impression that story and storying played a role in this. His life story did not appear as a resource or 'site' for learning. There was some evidence in the interviews of a consideration of alternative ways of being and living, but most of this was retrospective and clearly triggered by our questions.

We might say that John stuck *to* his script – which is different from saying that John was stuck *in* his script. To a large extent John's script 'worked' for the situations he found himself in. There was, in this regard, little reason for wanting to change his story. It fitted the particular 'ecology' of John's actions (see Biesta and Tedder 2007) – an ecology characterised by a significant degree of continuity and stability. Geographically, John stayed on the same farm most of his life, moving to live a few miles away only on semi-retirement. Socially his position remained stable. Psychically he tells of no great upheavals or traumas until the end of farming in 1995. It was only when the context of John's life began to change that a discrepancy began to occur between John's script and his life. John's world transformed whilst he tried to remain constant to the original script. There is considerable evidence that John tried to operate as if the world he grew up in was still present. He idealised a world where a shake of the hand or a nod of the head indicated that a 'gentleman's agreement' had been made. Throughout much of his farming life this was substantially true. But as market forces and land agents representing his landlord entered the scene this all changed with sudden and dramatic force. John was left adrift and without a programme of action in this new world. His birthright script was redundant but he was unpractised in script development since he was primarily used to following the script he had, a script that had served him very well for most of his life.

John Peel's case provides us with an example of someone for whom storying was not very important or prominent in how he lived his life. We have little doubt that John, up on the hills in his Land Rover with his dog by his side, on a crisp morning with the cows all around was filled with well-being. His case thus serves as an important reminder that people can lead good and fulfilling lives without narrative, without learning, and without narrative learning. While there may be little evidence of narrative learning in the case of John, the script that accompanied his life did serve him well and did offer him agentic opportunities within the particular ecology in which his life was lived. It was only when this ecology began to change that his story offered him little in terms of resources to engage with these changes through narrative and narration. This suggests that the more scripted kind of narrative, although a resource for agency within a particular ecology, offers relatively little in terms of flexibility. If we see the life narrative as a tool then John's case shows both the advantages and disadvantages of having a having a tool with less flexibility, a tool that is suited for particular tasks and circumstances but cannot easily be utilised in other situations.

## *Marie Tuck*

Initially the narrative of Marie Tuck, a woman in her mid-thirties who was married to a much older man with whom she had two children, a daughter aged six and a son aged two, was quite similar to that of John Peel. It was descriptive more than analytical, it was on the less elaborate end of the intensity spectrum, and initially did not give us many clues about any learning going on through narrative and narration. What makes Marie's case interesting – and also indicates the importance of the kind of longitudinal research we conducted – is that all this changed over time. As the project progressed – and as her life progressed – her stories became more elaborate, more analytical and more evaluative. It was as if, over time, Marie had become more familiar with the 'tool' of narrative and narration as an instrument for learning and understanding. In later interviews Marie revisited events in her life and deepened her account and understanding of them, focusing more on themes and issues that were troubling her and on the actions she had taken or was planning to take to make changes in her life. It could be that Marie had become more comfortable with the interview process and with the opportunities it provided for her to talk about and reflect upon her life. It certainly seemed serendipitous that the project interviews happened to coincide with a time when she needed to reflect on a major transition in her life.

The shift in the narrative quality of her stories was particularly apparent in the way in which a plot began to emerge, a plot that had to do with Marie's wish to be independent and in control of her life. This increasingly became the central theme and organising principle of Marie's narrative. The shift was most noticeably visible in the relationship with her husband, up to the point where, towards the end of the project, she made the decision to end her relationship with him. The plot not only provided structure and coherence in her life story but also appeared as a driving force in the way in which she accounted for her life and gave direction to it. Over time learning, identity and agency thus seemed to come together in Marie's life narrative.

When we compare Marie Tuck's case with that of John Peel perhaps the most significant difference between the two narratives is that whereas John Peel's life story was relatively finished and therefore lacked flexibility under changing circumstances, Marie's narrative was more 'in process' and under ongoing construction. There was no fixed 'script' to which Marie adhered in her storying, but a constant *contemporaneous* set of articulations and reflections. The main difference between John Peel's and Marie Tuck's narratives therefore lies in its flexibility rather than in its analytical depth. This appears to give Marie's narrative a greater efficacy, both at the level of learning and the level of action, in dealing with changing situations. Because it is contemporaneous and flexible, Marie's storying not only figures as a 'site' of reflection and learning, but as a 'site' of reflection and learning that clearly has an impact on action and agency.

## *Maggie Holman*

Maggie Holman, who at first interview was 49, had a capacity to tell very detailed, complex and sophisticated stories about her life. In this regard the quality of her narrative was clearly different from that of John Peel's or Marie Tuck's. Yet while there was high narrative intensity and also a strong plot – which had to do with the transition from being a graphic artist to being a wife and mother, something that gave Maggie a sense of purpose and direction in life – there was little analysis and reflection in Maggie's stories, although there were strong judgements. As a result it was difficult to gauge the extent to which any learning was occurring in and through the stories and the storying. When we discussed this more explicitly with Maggie towards the end of the project, she confirmed that she didn't believe that her stories were a vehicle for learning. Maggie felt that the stories she had told had actually shown how 'waffley' her life was. 'I mean if you're not doing, undergoing any formal learning, um it all becomes very waffley, and I feel all it does is to highlight how utterly waffley my life is anyway.'

One way in which Maggie's narration differed significantly from very many other participants in the project was that she didn't provide a chronological account of her life but rather one organised thematically. 'Colour' was one of the key themes in what Maggie had to say about her life. While many other participants described their lives in the form of a series of events and experiences occurring over time, Maggie rather provided us with scenes and pictures. Adding detail here was like 'zooming in' rather than extending and connecting in time. It was the pictorial quality of Maggie's stories and storying that eventually helped us to formulate a hypothesis about why an elaborate, emplotted and to a certain extent even theorised life story did not facilitate learning but did engender judgement. We surmised that while a chronological account makes it possible to consider relationships between actions and consequences and thus to evaluate one's actions in light of actual and possible consequences, this becomes far more difficult in the case of a 'pictorial' account. While there can be much detail in such accounts – and this is what makes Maggie's stories clearly different from those of John Peel's and Marie Tuck's – the detail does not highlight possible consequences for action and therefore may be less conducive to learning. Maggie's accounts were full of detail and complexity but lacked *sequentiality*. Maggie was able to 'zoom in' and 'zoom out' – as if working on a painting and trying to get foreground and background 'right' – but such as depiction does not work as a story that evolves and develops over time. This also helps to understand why, despite the absence of reflection and learning, Maggie did make (strong) judgements about the events in her life. Judgement here is about the ability to 'capture' and judge the scene as a whole, as a 'gestalt', we might say, in which the whole and the parts are organically connected. Maggie's case is therefore important for our understanding of narrative learning as it not only helps to see the importance of time, temporality and chronology in such learning, but also shows the specificity of narration as a form, site and process of learning from life.

## Diogenes

Diogenes – who worked for a charity that supports homeless people and was 59 at the time of our first encounter – proved to be an articulate participant able to talk at length during interviews that tended to last for around two hours. He talked eloquently about work and our interviews were able to monitor something of his response to the changes that took place in his life routine as his work role changed. Through this Diogenes provided stories with high narrative intensity and much analysis and evaluation. It was also clear, however, that he made a clear distinction between his public and private self in the stories he was prepared to tell. The power of his storytelling was directed in ways that he carefully controlled. He was forthcoming and expansive about his work role but needed questions to encourage him to talk about himself. He volunteered little about his family and saw little relevance in talking about them. Although he had been a widower since 1991, he said little about the nature of being in such a position.

Diogenes was able to talk about his experiences in both a personal and an academic framework. Interview transcripts include numerous references to historical events, particularly the Second World War, and Diogenes made sense of his experiences by setting them in a socio-historical context. He referred also to literary sources, to writers like Camus and Sartre, and to media sources as part of his cultural environment. In this regard Diogenes was one of the few respondents who presented us with a relatively theorised version of his life. The quality of analysis and reflection suggests that Diogenes had learned from his narrative – his critical political stance, for example, was the outcome of personal experience and theoretical reading that gave him tools for understanding the world and the tasks he undertook in it. The identifiable plot of Diogenes' narrative was a quest for greater social justice for homeless people. His continuing goal was to achieve a better deal, a better understanding in society for homeless people. He was angered by the indifference of others to the problems he encountered everyday and exasperated by the failure of the world to be more humane and more just.

Unlike in the cases discussed so far, Diogenes thus provided us with an example of someone whose life narrative was highly elaborate, emplotted, theorised and structured in a chronological more than a thematic manner. What also became clear from the conversations we had with him was that narrative and narration had helped him to learn from the events in his life and had given him a set of strong convictions, a strong normative outlook that helped him to navigate the present, and gave his life a sense of purpose and direction. In one respect, however, Diogenes was much closer to the case of John Peel in that we got the impression that much of his narrative learning had taken place in the past rather than that it was ongoing. While, unlike John Peel, his sense of self and the sense he made of his life was clearly the outcome of narrative learning, like John Peel the script he used to make sense of his life was less flexible then in the case of Marie Tuck. While there was, therefore, evidence of narrative learning there was less evidence of *ongoing* narrative learning. Within the particular 'ecology' of his life his 'script' suited him well and perhaps because the 'script' was less about who he was and more about what mattered to him it allowed for greater flexibility than in the case of John Peel. The identity of being a farmer may have less agentic possibilities than the identity of being a person concerned about social justice. There is one important proviso to be made: our analysis is exclusively based on what Diogenes was willing to share with us. For Diogenes there was a very clear distinction between his public story and his private story. As he made clear:

> I probably have said a few things that don't usually crop up in civilised conversation umm, and umm when you walk out the door that will be filed away back in the dark recess and left there, yeah. But bare my soul, no I haven't bared my soul, no, no. Oh no.

While Diogenes thus allowed us to gain an understanding of narrative learning in and through his public story there is very little we can say about what went on in his private story. His case thus stands as an important reminder about the specific nature of narrative data. They only give us access to *stories* about life and self, not to life and self in themselves.

### Christopher

Christopher was born in 1942 into a middle class family in southern England. He provides us with another example of someone whose life story is characterised by a high level of narrative intensity and where the predominant mode of narration is on the analytical and evaluative side of the spectrum much more than on the descriptive end. However, even in those cases where there are emplotted, analytical and evaluative stories with high narrative intensity, there are still important differences in terms of the learning potential – for example, compared to Diogenes, about whether the learning is completed or ongoing – and also with regard to the action potential. In contrast to Diogenes, Christopher presents us with narrative and narration that is much more an ongoing learning process; one, moreover, with a clear potential for action.

Christopher's stories were not only detailed and elaborate, they also had depth in that they were characterised by constant analysis, interpretation, sense-making and evaluation. For Christopher 'making sense' of his life, figuring out what is going on and why it is going on was an ongoing project. It is not something that was triggered by the interviews – although the interviews did provide him with additional opportunities for articulation and reflection – but was very much part of who Christopher is and how he continually was trying to make sense of his life. Although we might say that Christopher's life story has a clear plot – for example the conviction that there is a 'trajectory' as he called it, which is not an arbitrary choice about how to lead one's life but more like a kind of life theme that is there to be found and to be acted upon – what seems more appropriate here is to say that Christopher's narratives are characterised by ongoing emplotment. Indeed, in the very last interview Christopher began to reassess his identity as an artist and raised some deep questions about his sense of self and the direction of his life so far.

> I think I've used my whole art throughout my life, I've used it as an escape hatch, as a place to go when things got really hard. And I think in there has been, although I *do* think I have a *really*, a real vocation, I really think I have something to offer as an artist, I really do think I'm a true artist, I also think that through that I have actually missed out on a tremendous lot, or somehow sidestepped commitment to a lot of things that aren't to do with art... And it feels like a lot of all that needs to be assessed, the whole thing of what I've been doing with my life.

Ongoing emplotment not only means that Christopher is continually trying to make sense of his life and is trying to figure out what is going on – something that obviously requires analysis and evaluation. Through his narration he is also *creating* meaning and making his life meaningful. This means that Christopher's life story takes on a meaning unique to himself, although he draws on the scripts of others to weave his own yarns. There is not an 'off the peg' script that Christopher simply adopts; the life story is his unique creation and it is intimately connected with how he leads his life. In this regard his narrative is not simply retrospective and reflective; it is also prospective and proactive.

The kind of narration that Christopher has been involved in throughout his life – narration that is characterised by intensity and depth, analysis, reflection and judgement, and by ongoing emplotment – functions indeed as a 'site' for learning, that is, a site where Christopher tries to figure out what is going on and tries to make meaning out of his narrations and reflections. But Christopher's narration is not just a site for learning without consequences. Christopher does not only narrate the story; he also plans and acts. Christopher's is therefore an example of narration that not only has a high learning potential but also a high action potential. This partly has to do with the particular quality of his narration – the ongoing emplotment – yet it is also clear that this hangs together with his belief that there is a 'trajectory', that life is meaningful and that it is his task to find out what the meaning, plan and trajectory for him *is*. His narration both reflects and enacts this belief. Although Christopher's narrative has its own limitations it clearly illustrates how narrative learning can lead to the definition of a 'course of action'. In this case the course of action provided a whole pathway to vocational purpose and economic livelihood but it is more than that – it is an existential axis on which his whole life turns and in a real sense depends.

### *Paul Larsen*

In many respects the case of Paul Larsen, who was born in a rural area of Norway in 1949 and moved to England later on in his life, is very similar to that of Christopher. Here we have not only someone who constructs an enormously detailed account of life and self. The construction is also ongoing – an ongoing project of sense-making and meaning-making. Where the two cases begin to differ is with regard to the efficacy of narrative and narration. There is abundant evidence that Paul has learned and does learn from narrative and narration. Through the ways in which he has analysed his life, has reflected upon it and has constructed a story about his life, he has identified a central theme in his life, which is the search for a place where he can be himself. The way in which this theme functions as a plot in Paul's narration provides evidence of what he has learned from the reflective construction of his life narrative.

Although Paul seems to have identified the search for a place where he can be himself as the major theme in his life, this search is still ongoing. In one respect this is not surprising in that for many of us the task of achieving a sense of self is a lifelong project. But what is peculiar about Paul's case is the somewhat circular feeling to his narration, analysis and reflection. In a sense Paul continues to look for what he already knows rather than that he uses this knowledge to 'move on'. In terms of our analytical categories we might say that whereas the learning potential of Paul's narrative and narration seems to be high, the action potential is rather low. For some reason Paul's learning doesn't seem to translate into action.

While there may well be psychological explanations for this, our interest is whether this has anything to do with the characteristics of his narrative and narration. On the one hand we consider Paul to be one of the most sophisticated narrators we have interviewed. He seems almost to live 'in narration'. He is constantly rehearsing and recounting his story and seems to live within it. He also is highly proficient in formal learning milieux. He has completed a PhD late in life and throughout his life has enjoyed work in a wide range of learning genres broadening in spiritual and therapeutic zones of inquiry. Yet this overarching focus for all his searching and learning seems to block rather than promote (other) avenues of action and exploration of selfhood. There is in a sense *too much* narration, reflection and analysis in Paul's life and it is this that seems to inhibit opportunities to 'move on'. Paul seems imbued with narrativity. After three hours of narrating in interview 5, as the interview is being wound up, Paul comments: 'I never tire of this.' Constantly, he seems to want to make sense of himself and his world through telling his story. Yet Paul's narrative activity seems to have become an end in itself, rather than that he is utilising it as a means to draw consequences that allow for translation into action – and this may help to explain why the action potential of his narrative and narration remains underutilised.

With Paul Larsen we therefore have an example of a situation where narrative and narration clearly allow for learning but where this narrative learning does not translate into action because there is too much of it and because it seems to has become more an end in itself than a means for action. When raising the question about the action potential of narrative learning, the issue, therefore, is not whether there is narrative learning or not, but whether the learning is balanced. Paul's case thus helps us to see that narrative activity can also get in the way of action.

### Eva

Eva, a musician born in 1971 in a Transylvanian city in Romania, the daughter of a Catholic Hungarian father and a Jewish Hungarian mother, both musicians, also provided us with a life narrative characterised by high narrative intensity. Eva's life story went beyond the simple description of her life. She explained and evaluated, weaving into her story the story of others including aspects of the socio–cultural–political context in which her life had been lived. She was highly articulate and there is evidence that she is highly reflective. Moreover, being reflective is clearly part of her sense of self. It's not only the way she 'is' – it's also the way in which she understands herself.

> I suppose because I'm the sort of person who always examines what I just did, erm, erm, I do find myself examining other people's behaviour as well so that I can then draw a conclusion from it, because it is, it is a conscious process, of course it's also an unconscious process.

The ongoing reflection about herself and her life, about her choices and the things that have crossed her path, work as a plot within Eva's story. She recounts her life and the events in it through the lens of her emerging and ongoing self-understanding and self-reflection. Eva not only creates a story that helps to explain and make sense of her life but also creates a narrative and develops narration that provides her with a focus on her sense of self. The process is one of both learning about her self and at the very same time constructing and reconstructing her self. She continually stories other ways of being and creates or seizes opportunities that allow these strategies to travel the route of their creation. Whilst drawing on scripts available in her social cultural spheres she weaves them into a mosaic of her own making.

Eva thus presents us with an example of someone with ongoing narrative learning 'in action' and the focus of the learning is very much on the self. We wouldn't want to characterise this mode of narrative learning as 'self-centred' or even 'self-obsessed' as Eva's ongoing reflections on who she is and who she can be clearly have a function in relation to the events in her life. Within Eva's story there is both stability and instability. Stability may be seen in the form of a continuation of the familial script taking as her life path the career of musician. There was a stability of a kind provided in her childhood through a very structured educational system in Romania, particularly one that provided opportunities for gifted musicians, but there was also instability. As a teenager she was uprooted from her home to begin a new life in Israel and whilst this has been storied positively as a new beginning there were clearly hardships connected with this and with her preceding family life in Romania. Through choice she subsequently moved to London and whilst this has provided her with opportunities to develop a musical career it has also been a further stage of uprooting and re-establishment. Through the various transitions in her life Eva has been able to follow a plot built around her identity as a musician. Whilst the form of musicianship has changed in various ways, this has provided the central spine of her story. As a person constantly living 'in narration' and highly reflective and analytical she is able to 're-self' in each new incarnation or context. This provides her with flexibility to respond to the new situations and opportunities that confront her and it is in this way that Eva's case provides important insights for the ways in which and conditions under which this form of narrative learning with its strong focus on self and identity can actually support agency.

### Russell Jackson

Russell was aged 53 when we first met, and a married man. He identified with the part of the country where he was born and has a strong local accent. He was a willing interviewee, someone with strong views and deep emotions to express, and someone accustomed to self-evaluation. He often referred to himself in humorous, slightly self-deprecating terms. His was a first person narrative, a candid account of actions and decisions that he took and of events over which it would seem he had no control, such as a conversion experience that set him out on a trajectory of becoming a priest. He was not only able to describe key events in his life but also to elaborate on their significance and meaning for him. It was quickly apparent that reflection on experience was a central feature of Russell's narrative, something he undertook in the interviews and also reported happening at other times and in other places in his life. Russell's stories were thus characterised by a high level of narrative intensity. They were detailed and elaborate and more on the analytical and evaluative than descriptive end of the spectrum. In this regard they were quite similar to the stories told by Christopher and Paul Larsen.

Russell's stories were characterised by the presence of a strong plot. The plot of his life story was his 'core identity' of being a priest, which, for Russell, signified the crucial importance of wanting to make a contribution to the well-being of others. Although in one respect Russell recounted his life in a chronological order, the identity of being a priest was the centre from which all events in his life gained their meaning. It also provided the criterion against which all events in his life were evaluated. With each aspect of Russell's life story there was always the question – sometimes explicitly posed, sometimes more implicitly alluded to – how it either brought him closer to this core identity or moved him further away from it. The plot in Russell's narrative thus not only served as an organising principle; at the very same time it functioned as an *evaluative* and *justificatory* principle.

Recognition of the central importance of this plot was clearly something that he had learned from his life – through a complex process of experience, reflection, communication and interaction – and it was something that not only had significant impact on his life as an 'event' (it led, for example, to his decision to give up his job, sell his house and train as a priest); it also had a significant impact on the *perception* of his life and hence on the way in which he was able to make sense of his life and of himself. Russell's narrative is not simply a descriptive account of a succession of life events. It has a strong *evaluative* character in that life events are positioned and evaluated in relation to what is most central and most important for him.

When we ask what kind of opportunities for learning and action Russell's narratives provided, we can therefore conclude that the plot was a major device for Russell's narrative learning. Unlike with Christopher, whose narrative learning was more a process of ongoing emplotment and re-emplotment, the plot that functioned in Russell's story remained relatively stable. Whereas Christopher developed an idea of a sense of trajectory fairly early on in his life and spent the rest of his life in search of the trajectory, with Russell the sense of direction emerged at some point in his life – and in Russell's narrative it was presented as a conversion experience – and from then on became his trajectory and a reference point for reflection, evaluation, learning and action. Russell's insights into what mattered most to him thus provided him with a criterion for making decisions at important transition points in his life – and it is in this way that his narrative learning 'translated' into action and provided him with agency. This is not to suggest that Russell was in total control of his life – on the contrary, his life is full of events that happen to him rather than that he actively chose them. Yet it is the way in which Russell responded to such events that helps to understand how the action potential of Russell's narrative learning was achieved – a learning that did not simply come to an end, such as in the case of Diogenes, but remained ongoing as a constantly available source for reflection and action. On Russell's own account storytelling did indeed play an important role in all this.

> I'm not well qualified. I'm not, you know, hugely intelligent or all those really worthwhile things, I've just got a story. And the story informs who I am and the story makes me who I am and out of that I have an ability and a confidence and the ability to deal with people in their stories.

## Conclusions: towards a theory of narrative learning

Our case studies leave us with a complex ecology of narratives and narration as would be expected in such an intricate and intimate aspect of human activity. Some of the distinctions that emerge from our studies are important in theorising narrative learning.

The key distinction that emerges is that between the use of life *narratives* as tools for learning, agency and identity construction and the ongoing process of *narration* itself as a site for learning. What all our cases show, but is particularly highlighted by Maggie Holman and Diogenes, albeit for different reasons, is that the employment of life narratives as tools can exist in an intensive and active manner without the presence of ongoing and pervasive narration activity. It would seem from our research that while most people do recount life stories when interviewed, not everybody works with narration as an ongoing internal conversation or external accounting mechanism. Narrative learning then, appears to take place in two ways. First, such learning can take place by the employment of life narratives as tools for facilitating learning. Second, such learning can take place at the site of narration itself, through the ongoing internal conversation and external accounts that are undertaken as a genuinely lifelong process. From this angle narrative learning appears to be maximal when evidenced both at the site of the life narrative as a tool and at the site of ongoing narration. There is, however, a complex ecology to narrative learning. As we have shown, not everybody learns in this way and there are considerable personal variations.

Our case studies indicate that the maximal capacity for narrative learning is reached when life narratives as tools and narration as ongoing activity are active and in a productive balance. In such cases – Christopher, Eva, Russell Jackson – the learning potential and action potential are substantially explored. We might see this as type of *open* narrative learning where all the channels for learning are open. As we have said before, the case of Paul Larsen is significant in that whilst the narrative learning is highly intense and the learning potential considerable, the action potential is not fully explored. Likewise in the case of John Peel we see the development of a life story based on established socially recognised scripts but with virtually no ongoing narration. This is a *closed* form of narrative learning with virtually no channel between narrative and narration. As a result the flexibility of response to new life experiences and events is diminished. Diogenes also represents a closed model where the narrative is a finished product, a final script almost, with no *ongoing* narration or modification albeit that in his case it is the strength of the convictions stemming from his narrative learning that allow him to operate effectively in different contexts and under different circumstances. In Marie Tuck's case we see in fascinating detail the transition from closed narrative learning to open narrative learning. The balance of narrative as static tool through to ongoing narration and narrative reformulation changes dramatically. In this case we see the move to narrative learning in action. There the culminating process is open, flexible, a work in progress.

Our case studies leave us with a complex ecology of narratives and narration as would be expected in such an intricate and intimate aspect of human activity. Some of the distinctions that emerge from our studies are important in theorising narrative learning.

The key distinction that emerges is that between the use of life narratives as tools for learning, agency and identity construction and the ongoing process of narration itself as a site for learning. What all our cases show , but is particularly highlighted by Maggie and Diogenes, albeit for different reasons, is that the first category, employment of life narratives as tools, can exist in an intensive and active manner without the presence of ongoing and pervasive narration activity. It would seem from our studies that while most people do recount life stories when interviewed, not everybody works with narration as an ongoing internal conversation or external accounting mechanism. Narrative learning, then, appears to take place in two ways. First, learning can take place by the employment of life narratives as tools for facilitating learning strategies. Second, learning can take place at the site of 'narration' itself, through the ongoing internal conversation and external accounts that are undertaken as a genuinely lifelong process. From this angle narrative learning is maximal when evidenced both at the site of the life narrative as a tool and at the site of ongoing narration. There is, however, a complex ecology to narrative learning. As we have shown, not everybody learns in this way and there are considerable personal variations.

Our case studies indicate that the maximal capacity for narrative learning is reached when life narratives as tools and narration as ongoing activity are active and in a productive balance. In these cases – Christopher, Eva, Russell Jackson – the learning potential and action potential are substantially explored. We might see this as type of *open* narrative learning where all the channels for learning are open. The key issue in theorising narrative learning is the issue of balance between the various aspects and dimensions. As we have said before, the case of Paul is significant in that whilst the narrative learning is highly intense and the learning potential considerable, the action potential is not fully explored. Likewise in the case of John Peel we see the development of a life story based on established socially recognised scripts but with virtually no ongoing narration. This is a *closed* form of narrative learning with virtually no channel between the narrative and narration. As a result the flexibility of response to new life experiences and events is diminished. Diogenes also represents a closed model where the narrative is a finished product, a final script almost, with no ongoing narration or modification although in his case it is the 'strength' of the convictions that stem from his narrative learning that allow him to operate in different contexts and under different circumstances, but at the risk of becoming cynical about those situations. In Marie Tuck's case we see in fascinating detail the transition from closed narrative learning to open narrative learning. The balance of narrative as static tool through to ongoing narration and narrative reformulation changes dramatically. In this case we see the move to narrative learning in action. There the culminating process is open, flexible, a work in progress.

At its best narrative learning thus provides an interesting dimension of learning through the lifecourse, for the development of a nuanced and flexible response to the challenges and changes that life brings. But it is important not to forget that narrative learning is neither a necessary nor a sufficient condition for leading a happy and rewarding life. Narrative learning is a highly personal form of learning. It is one that people can decide to engage in more explicitly or not, but it is not something that can or should be demanded from anyone, not should it be seen as a panacea for the problems that educational institutions are currently faced with. Narrative learning belongs to the domain in which, as Carl Rogers (1969) has put it, individuals have a freedom to learn – which, by definition, implies that they also have the freedom not to learn.

# Chapter 5

# The role of generations

## Introduction: generations in our lives

In this chapter we focus on the role of generations in understanding learning through the lifecourse. The notion of 'generation' refers, on the one hand, to family positions and relationships and thus marks off phases of the lifecourse in terms of being a child, parent or grandparent. And the notion of 'generation as cohort' encapsulates a broader socio-economic outlook as an age-based form of social identification that is structured around people's shared experiences and understandings and the specific social and political events that have occurred throughout their lifecourse. In both cases, learning plays an important role. Family contexts form an intimate and immediate environment for informal learning, which then has enormous spillover effects into education and training throughout life; and every age cohort is influenced by the education and training that its members receive, and they in turn bring shared generational dispositions to bear upon their understandings of what learning is and can be in their lives.

Research into cohort-based generational groupings has its roots in sociology. In what is now a classic point of reference, Karl Mannheim (1952) drew comparisons between generational bonding and class solidarity. For Mannheim, it was important to distinguish between the shared objective conditions of a cohort and their subjective consciousness of a shared interest based on age. In recent years educational researchers have paid considerable attention to generational analysis (see, for example, Antikainen et al. 1996; Alheit 2003; Olkinuora et al. 2008; Ecclestone et al. 2009), with a particular but not exclusive focus on generational differences in experiences of the education and training system in relation to such dimensions as the ways in which the education system itself has changed (for example the raising of the school leaving age), the importance of external influences on education (for example the disruption caused by war), and the ways in which the system relates to its immediate environment (which include transformation in family structures, or sharp variations in the youth labour market).

Again, these ideas are often found throughout our culture. There is, for example, widespread recognition and use of terms such as 'baby boomers' (used generally of people born between 1945 and the early 1960s) and Generation X (born mid-1960s to late 1970s). Conventionally, the two are contrasted sharply. Boomers came of age at a time of post-war political optimism, economic prosperity, social change, technological innovation and of challenges to previously established social and racial inequalities. As many popular novels and films confirm, many of these developments were at the sharpest and most visible inside the universities, whose students and later graduates were supposedly characterised by their iconoclasm, idealism and investment in permanent youthfulness, and their strong sense of collective identity born of rock music, social movements, fashion and consumption. Generation X, by contrast, are perceived as sceptical individualists who came of age surrounded by economic uncertainty, the decline of the welfare consensus, rapid expansion of higher education intakes, and the computerisation of everyday life; there was extensive cynicism about the supposed benefits of education, particularly higher education, with the popular media routinely attacking 'Mickey Mouse degrees' (McMullin et al. 2007). Such notions of generation appear to play a valuable role in popular culture as sources of humour, pride, recognition and both positive and negative identification. So it is not surprising if our interviewees also share many of these ideas, and plot them into their narratives.

## Talking about 'my generation'

Many of the participants in the Learning Lives project spontaneously used the idea of 'generation' to talk about their life (see also Field 2008). Some spoke explicitly of generations as a way of signalling continuities between past and future. Archie Bone, a coal miner in his late fifties at the time of the interviews, connected his narrative with a broader family history when he pointed out that 'five generations of our family goes back in the mining industry'. When an injury led him to retire he undertook local historical research into a mining disaster. After publishing a short book on the episode, Archie then started to campaign for a memorial to the dead miners, so as to 'have something there lasting to let future generations know'. Archie took education seriously as an intergenerational project, volunteering to speak in local schools about the area's history, and telling young people of his own early life as a coal miner. He, and others, spoke of generation as a form of community.

By contrast with those who plotted generations as continuity, some younger interviewees used generational notions of time to distinguish themselves from people belonging to earlier or later cohorts. The young

woman who chose 'Brother Raphael' as her pseudonym was very much
the daughter of a 'sixties mum'. She spoke of the strong state education
that her parents had enjoyed, adding that 'they were the first generation
to be able to do that'. She described her father as affectionate but
reserved, which she saw as a product of the fact that 'he was just from
a different generation', in which men were unaccustomed to expressing
intimacy. Helena Johnstone, an adult educator in her thirties, deliberately
used signals of youth such as 'cool' during her interviews. Like Brother
Raphael, she contrasted herself with earlier generations, joking that 'I've
been lucky that I've come from a generation where you didn't marry
the first guy that you got together with'. Jeannie Taylor, a call centre
manager in her mid-thirties, referred to the poor IT skills of workers from
'generally the older generation', though she saw them as potentially good
call centre workers nevertheless, because their experience gave them
greater resilience.

Some older interviewees also drew contrasts between the generations.
Billy Milroy, a Glaswegian ex-prisoner in his forties who was persuaded to
take a course in order to improve his employability, initially reacted badly
when he found his fellow students included a mixture of 'people that didn't
go to school and the older generation like people of my parents' age'. Only
when he struck up a relationship with his numeracy teacher did he decide
to stay the course. While for Billy the idea of generation mainly served as
a negative marker that signalled a difference between him and his fellow
students, Archie used it to signal inter-generational continuity, providing
him with a language that allows him to explore the relationship that he
desired with those who were younger than himself.

Some interviewees used the language of generations to depict both
difference and community. Lui Carter, born to Pakistani parents, used the
term to draw attention to what he shared with other British-born Pakistanis,
as well as what they did not share with their parents. He used this to
contrast his values and identity with those of his parents' generation:

> I'm probably the first generation of, you know, British Asian children
> that have been born and brought up in the UK, so that in itself is a
> completely new, different experience, we see and address things and
> view things differently from how our parents did.

By contrast, he described how his mother and father were aliens in
Britain: they had, he said,

> come over to a completely alien country to them and are bringing
> up their own next generation children up as they remember being
> brought up so many years ago. What they fail to understand or realise
> though that the land that they grew up in has also changed and it's

evolved and it's not how they remember it, so really they're alien here, well they feel alien here.

Lui saw himself 'as a first generation Asian Brit as they call it', who had none of his parents' certainty about nation and religion as sources of identity. His identity was, he thought, a source of ambiguity and uncertainty, where:

> what we're trying to do in my generation is trying to maintain the peace and respect of our parents and understanding, you know, respect of the family and the honour and not bringing on shame, you're torn between that and the life that you're really leading which is living in the western open-minded world where things aren't as suppressed and frowned upon as they are back in India or Pakistan or wherever.

Within the family circle, generational time was a frequent point of reference for interviewees, who used generational positions and events as key, easily understood markers of identity and change. Cohort membership was treated in a more diffuse way, and was cited partly in order to draw a contrast between one's own peers and members of a younger or older cohort. In both cases, generation could also be a reference point for explaining learning. People contrasted their own experiences and expectations with those of their parents, and with those of their own children. They also associated shared educational experiences, such as university study or youth training schemes, both with their identity and their hopes for the future.

Some sociologists suggest generational identities are assuming increasing importance in people's lives. In a contingent, late modern social order, where categories such as class or even gender have become more fluid, Martin Kohli suggests that for some, at least, generation constitutes an increasingly important framework for living our individual lives, and also acquires greater significance as a collective anchoring for our social identity (Kohli 2003: 4). Heinz Bude suggests that while people can deliberately change their class or even their gender, it is harder to find ways of escaping from one's age cohort; he also notes that the idea of generation, lacking the political baggage of class and the historical associations of nation, may hold an active appeal as a positive pole of identification (Bude 2000: 19–20). Equally, as we have seen, it may provide an attractive negative pole. People develop an identity through what they do not share with others, as well as what they do share; and again the relatively 'clean' associations of generation may mean that people are comfortable with identifying themselves as *not* belonging to 'today's youth' or 'the old sixty-eighters'. Whether it is of growing significance or not, though, generational experiences play an important part in people's understanding of the self, and educational experiences appear to be critical to these understandings of generation.

## Learning generations

Generational relationships, in both of the senses distinguished above, provide one element in the complex ecology of narratives and narration by which people tell the story of their lives. It can also be seen as comprising part of the varied web of relationships that constitute position and shape dispositions (see Chapter 6 for further discussion of these concepts). People often speak of generation in association with skills, knowledge and schooling. Jeannie Taylor, in the example cited above, portrayed older workers in her call centre as typically having poor IT skills combined with strong broad experience of the world. Lui Carter talked evocatively of his generation of British Asians as people who have learned values and habits from their English or Scottish peers, while his parents' generation had learned how to cope as migrants in a new environment while preserving values that they had brought with them from Pakistan. Several people spoke, like Kathleen Donnelly, of the generation who had been at school with them.

Narrated generations often, then, possess a clear educational dimension. It is not just that people feel bound together by shared experiences of particular periods of schooling; they also highlight differences from other generations' experiences. Kathleen Donnelly, a youth worker in her forties who originally came from a manual worker milieu, had been taken aback by the behaviour of the younger generation: 'meeting the up and coming generation, it's shocking, really shocking, I'm shocked to the core what actually goes on in society'. She also contrasted the educational careers of her own age group with those of older family members: 'you can see the difference in the generations like from my granny, my mum, to like me and my sisters'. Later on, she spoke about her aim of improving life for members of her own daughter's generation, remarking that

> I feel as though my generation's been lost, really lost, I know it's dead easy to blame Margaret Thatcher and the Tory administration and all that, but it's been lost, there's a lost generation out there where my friends, the friends I used to hang about at school with, are heroin addicts and stuff like that.

The question, then, is whether people's understandings of generational attachments lead them to adopt shared dispositions towards learning. To answer this requires us first to clarify some of the basic terminology. Most definitions of generation tend to follow Mannheim, but even so most generational categories tend to be rather broad, and their boundaries are fuzzy. As an example, let us take the definition offered by Antikainen and colleagues in their discussion of educational generations in Finland.

> A generation consists of a group of people born during the same time period and who are united by similar life experiences and a temporarily coherent cultural background. People belonging to the same generation have the same location in the historical dimension of the social process.
>
> (Antikainen et al. 1996: 34)

This begs some obvious questions. Precisely which 'time period', for example? And how temporary, and how coherent, is the cultural background? How can these broad generalisations be turned into categories that help us understand the meanings that people attach to generational belonging?

The most common approach in the literature is to define generations in terms of birth cohorts. Some, though, suggest that birth cohort and nation together are likely to create similar experiences at similar ages/stages of life (Hammarström 2004). Typical is an Australian study of generation and identity that took the Boomer generation as a 'watershed' (Phillips and Western 2005). The authors produced a tripartite categorisation grouped around this pivotal cohort: (1) The Baby Boom cohort, born 1946–1960; (2) pre-Boom, born before 1946; (3) Post-Boom, born after 1960 (Phillips and Western 2005: 173). Interestingly, drawing on survey data, the authors found relatively little difference between the self-identities of the three groups, which perhaps confirms the difficulties of defining boundaries in terms of birth cohorts.

Some other researchers prefer not to use birth cohorts as the basis of generational analysis, but rather to look at the years when people came of age, passing through adolescence and early adulthood. Alanen adopts what she calls a structuralist approach, defining generation as 'a socially constructed system of relationships among social positions in which children and adults are the holders of specific social positions defined in relation to each other and constituting, in turn, specific social (and in this case generational) structures' (Alanen 2001: 12). But this still begs the question, to use Mannheim's terminology, of whether we can then distinguish actual (subjectively felt) generations from potential (structurally defined) generations. While a strong relational element is highly plausible, and structural factors are certainly a necessary precondition, we also need to look for shared experiences and a degree of cultural unity as further conditions of any definition of generational groupings.

This is particularly significant when we come to consider learning and generation. The relationship between generation and learning has a long history in educational thinking, principally in terms of inter-generational transfers of knowledge and values so that children acquired the abilities to function in their parents' society (Eccarius 2002). This 'classical' view of inter-generational socialisation as a one-way process, where the adult generations teach the young, has its roots in antiquity and survived the modernisation processes until relatively recent times. Some now suggest that 'inverse socialisation' – defined as the transfer of knowledge and skills from children to their parents – has become a marked feature of the information society (Cochinaux and Woot 1995); and indeed we may add the transfer of values and lifestyles from adolescents to adults, where some parents try to retain the lifestyle of the perpetual teenager. These processes can be overlaid with more or less overt conflict between generations, material as well as cultural. McMullin et al. (2007: 308) noted that many of the younger IT workers in their sample thought that their generations tended simply to 'pick up' computing skills, believing that older ones had to work at it; their interviewees routinely used the language of generations, sometimes with slightly abusive overtones ('old farts', 'young idiots').

The place of education in the narratives illuminates the complexity of relations over time between people's learning and the rest of their lives. Almost all of the older adults told stories involving strict teachers. Archie Bone, a coal miner who had gone to school in the 1930s and early 1940s, wove a wider pattern into his account when he recalled the military background of his head teacher.

> The local school that we went to isn't there any longer, it was knocked doon a long number of years ago, and we had a headmaster that was called Captain Gracy, he had been a captain in the army, and he turned to education when he was invalided out the army and he was a very, very hard taskmaster.

The headteacher inspected every child for cleanliness and neatness, and sent errant children to wash or brush their shoes before entering the classroom.

For Archie Bone, the transition to secondary school brought another unsettling experience: he had to travel into Stirling and home again by bus, which 'was like going into London, you were just lost, there was masses and masses of houses and people busy running about all over the place, and we weren't used to that'. So school was a doubly disorienting experience, which Archie saw as tending to dislodge him from his own *tight-knit* community.

For Brother Raphael, a favourable disposition towards learning was part of family cultural capital:

> My parents had been to university but they were smart and they had a very open disposition to knowledge and reading in quite an old-fashioned cultural way because both were quite religious and they'd

both had a classical education and which they'd both won by being super smart and they were also the first generation to be able to do that.

Similarly at school, where her own reading and cultural taste had made her aware of 'all these divvy girls, I suddenly realised the social politics of that, about nice girls going on to uni'. She became 'this arty girl' as a reaction against the kind of quite repressive regime at home, with a strong imaginary vision of arts school:

> I'm talking about the cultural narratives, I'm talking about how like being into a certain sort of music, be into David Bowie and being into culture and narrative of what an art school was, cause I thought oh, that, you know, I kind of saw it from the distance like somewhere glowing, but it wasn't that there was a canon, it was that that was a place, it was like it was a world, it was like a utopia, it was like in music.

She did poorly at secondary school in a middle class rebel kind of way, passing three higher grades instead of the six that her family had expected; so instead of going to one of the Scottish art schools, she went to Chelsea for a year, became pregnant and went back to Scotland with her baby daughter. Once her daughter was in school, Brother Raphael went to arts school, working mainly with textiles, taking an MA while also caring for her now elderly parents.

Discipline, which we have seen in the stories of the older adults, also featured in the memories of some interviewees who had been born in the sixties. Carmen, born in 1963 to a lower middle class family, went to Catholic schools, and strict discipline was again part of her account. Even at primary school, 'I can remember, there were a couple of teachers who were very strict, very old school, and, you know, the chalk flying, rulers flying, the belt...' She lived 200 metres away from a non-denominational school, but 'the diocese for the church dictated where you went', and she bussed to a Catholic secondary school, where some of the classes were taken by nuns. Some of the teachers also taught in a neighbouring boys' school, 'so I then had teachers who were used to teaching boys and belting them left, right and centre, and shouting and screaming a lot'. Daisy Paterson, born in 1964 into a mining family, 'was always getting my knuckles slapped wi' the ruler, "Oh, you write properly."' While her family encouraged Carmen to pursue higher education, neither of her parents had been to university, and her mother – a secretary – in particular 'was quite bitter about her lack of opportunity, so probably quite aware that I had better opportunities'. Daisy Paterson had just completed an Open University (OU) foundation course at the time of her second interview and already held two Scottish Vocational Qualifications (SVQs) that she had taken since leaving school. However, she needed a higher education qualification to become a qualified social worker, and during the first interview she was finding the OU course heavy going. Even after finishing it, she said, 'I'm not a fabulous studier and I'm not clever at revising.'

So here again we can see generational specificities in adults' educational experiences. For older adults school was a place of discipline and harshness, a shocking breach with the rules that governed the previously known world of home and community. Higher education was simply not an option. For the younger group, higher education was the normal pathway for middle class adults, an abnormal pathway for Daisy, and a no entry road for Andy Lawson , a skilled engineer who had 'hated school' and saw any off-the-job learning as 'the easy route'; he had left school at sixteen to work with his dad. This is not to adopt generational determinism: Brother Raphael was a refusenik in this respect as in so many others, and viewed the expectations of her social milieu with great suspicion. But people from different generations were confronted with different expectations and possibilities in education as in other aspects of their lives.

## Defining learning generations

Several studies have examined the relationship between generations and education. A number of Finnish studies have become particularly influential in recent years, particularly since the publication in English of a landmark study by Ari Antikainen and his colleagues (Antikainen et al. 1996). Accepting that of course there are huge variations in the experiences of different socio-economic groups and between those of the genders, different generational cohorts have distinctive experiences of the education and training system both in their youth and subsequently, in early adulthood and later in their lifecourse. Examples include changes inside the education system itself (such as the raising of the school leaving age), those that are external (such as the disruption caused by the world wars of the twentieth century), and those that concern the system's relationship with its immediate environment (which include transformation in family structures, or sharp variations in the youth labour market). For a variety of historical reasons, these changes have been unusually sharp in Finland, leading some researchers to conclude that 'the educational gaps between different age groups are very wide in international comparison' (Olkinuora et al. 2008: 42). This distinctive generational pattern may mean that the Finnish case is atypical, but the existence of a body of related studies is nevertheless significant for researchers working in different European contexts.

In their study, Antikainen and colleagues identified four generational groupings (1996: 35). How they did so is not entirely clear from their account. The four categories appear to be based on relational and historical factors, and in three cases are defined by their shared educational experiences:

- Cohort with little generation (born before 1935).
- Cohort of educational growth and inequality (1936–1945).
- Cohort of educational growth and welfare (1946–1965).
- Young people (1966–).

The last grouping is anomalous, in that it is initially defined by relative age rather than relationship to the educational system. The study is particularly concerned with considering the different orientations of each cohort to the possibility of learning in adult life.

A similar approach has been adopted by a group of researchers from the University of Turku (Aro et al. 2005). Basing their analysis empirically on a large-scale survey of adult education participation in Finland, this group also distinguishes between four groups:

- The cohort of war and scarce education (born 1921–1939).
- Structural changes and growing educational opportunities (1940–1955).
- Welfare and abundant educational choices (1956–1969).
- Forced individual choices (1970–1982).

The fourth generation is described as facing 'not only the freedom but also the necessity of continuous choices', arising partly from marketisation, with pupils being portrayed as clients faced with a variety of curricular options (Aro et al. 2005: 465). As with the Antikainen study, the survey data confirmed that there are clear differences between generations in attitudes towards learning; while all cohorts placed a high value on formal education, older adults tended to see it as a guaranteed pathway to social mobility, while younger adults tended to view it as a necessary, but not a sufficient, condition for employment and a career (Aro et al. 2005: 472). Again, then, this suggests that the concept of educational or learning generations has some warrant in the evidence.

A third study, also by researchers from Turku, draws on the work of Antikainen, Aro and Roos among others (Olkinuora et al. 2008). Based on a large body of empirical data gathered between the mid-1980s and the early years of this century, it examines the meanings of lifelong learning for three generational cohorts:

- Young adults (20–35 years old), facing forced individual choices as a result of insecurity in the labour market combined with the steady extension of initial education.
- Middle-aged workers/citizens (35–50 years old), who experienced welfare and wide educational choice in their youth, and overwhelmingly work in secure employment.

- Aged adults and pensioners (aged over 50), who share very strong beliefs in the value of education, but are themselves often on the periphery of the learning and information society (see Olkinuora et al. 2008: 44–53).

These authors conclude that a 'participation threshold' has arisen between the oldest generation, who are unlikely neither to have opportunities to learn nor particularly wish to take up those that are available, and younger generations, who may take these opportunities for granted (Olkinuora et al. 2008: 55).

All of these Finnish models seek to connect generational groupings to shared experiences of education, connecting private experiences with changes in public institutions. They may require modification, though, in a number of ways. There is, for example, evidence of a marked gender dimension to educational generations. In their qualitative study of three generations of Norwegian women, for example, Bjerrum Nielsen and Monica Rudberg (2000) note that for those whose youth occurred in the period 1955–1965, getting away from their mothers' lives is often an explicit aim, while education has become available as an *obvious choice*. For this group's own daughters, aged around eighteen at the time of the study, higher education is no longer an obvious choice, but rather a requirement, needed in order to realise one's skills and abilities. For the authors, university study had thus become an obligatory component in the 'project of individualization'.

Of course, the gap between genders is not necessarily a sharply defined one. Bettina Dausien stresses that biographical differences between men and women fall into patterns that are better described as 'gender-typical' rather than 'gender-specific' (Dausien 1998: 108). These typical patterns themselves may be changing, not least as a result of declining average family sizes (including significant growth in the number of no-child units) and steady rises the proportions of time spent by women in paid employment. Nevertheless, within these 'typical' narrative patterns, women show more of a tendency to present and assess their biographies in terms of relationships, particularly kinship relations and community ties but also increasingly workplace connections, while men are more likely to focus on their self as agent, acting primarily throughout their work trajectory (Dausien 1998: 11–13). The marked gender dimension to generation is particularly important in view of the 'opening up' of the educational space to women during the course of the twentieth century. Further, there is a well-known tendency for education to play a greater part in shaping life chances for women than it does for men (see for example Blundell et al. 2000).

## Why learning generations matter

What does generation have to do with learning? Like many later commentators, Mannheim thought that events and experiences in youth were particularly important in generational formation. This was a stage of life when people experienced 'fresh contact' with the 'accumulated heritage' (Mannheim 1952: 293) and responded in the light of their own understandings rooted in their own historical location. As well as freshness, this life stage is widely thought of as crucial in the process of identity formation, and is characterised by high levels of contact with like-aged peers across a variety of contexts (McMullin et al. 2007: 302–303). Potentially, then, this suggests that education may be a particularly significant feature of generational formation.

There are at least five ways in which age cohorts can become 'educational generations'. First, school structures and cultures primarily affect the young, and therefore form a central part of the generational habitus during youth. Second, since the structures and cultures of school systems are subject to change, they are therefore 'something that has an effect on what a generation takes for granted' that then distinguishes it from other cohorts (Aro et al. 2005: 461). Third, school systems are connected with other areas of everyday life, and particularly with people's transitions into adulthood. They therefore shape people's experiences of the labour market, and they tend to influence – and feature strongly in – people's accounts of their subsequent adult lives. This aspect is strongly associated with the ways in which people's identities are formed (including self-forming of identity). Fourth, school systems can trigger cohort-based social movements. The clearest example in recent decades is probably the student movement of the late 1960s and early 1970s, which provides a widely recognised generational marker. Finally, generations may have shared dispositions that lead to a positive or negative stance towards lifelong learning. For example, baby boomers who see themselves as 'forever young' are likely to see enthusiasm about learning as an expression of their youthful orientation towards life.

So what can we learn from the existing body of knowledge? In particular, the Finnish studies indicate that there are some important differences between generations in their attitudes towards both initial education and adult learning. Some of this is common sense: for instance, being a university student is likely to have carried a very distinctive set of meanings for young people at a time when the higher education participation rate was three per cent; the same status carries quite different meanings when the participation rate is over 40 per cent, and higher education entry is part of the normal biography – at least for the middle classes, for girls and for some ethnic groups. But some of these studies have found much more deeply rooted differences in orientations towards learning, resulting for example in varying generational views of on-the-job-training (Aro et al. 2005: 466).

Table 5.1 represents a preliminary attempt to categorise educational generations in contemporary Britain. There are important national differences in education systems within Britain; in particular, the early introduction of comprehensive secondary education in Scotland, and its continuing dominance, mean that educational generations may not be as clearly distinguished as in England and Wales, and this affects cohorts who entered secondary school after the Second World War. It is not just that the school systems themselves therefore provide different experiences, but they also have different consequences; in particular, school leaver attainment in Scotland tends to be higher on average, much less affected by school characteristics, and – perhaps most significantly – shows a relatively small gap between high achievers and low achievers, particularly compared with England (Raffe 2008). In many other respects, such as the breakdown of existing transition-to-work systems in the 1970s, the rapid expansion of higher education in the 1980s/1990s, and the expansion of early years education, the differences between Britain's three national systems are relatively minor.

Methodologically, even broad generational groupings of this nature are open to challenge. As Paterson and Iannelli note, the analysis of cohort-based evidence is liable to bias arising from differential mortality and migration (Paterson and Iannelli 2007: 336). While they are particularly concerned with the limitations for quantitative data sets, this inbuilt bias can also be an issue for researchers working on qualitative data, such as those used in this study. So while our work does pick up on experiences of individual people from immigrant backgrounds, whose initial schooling took place outside of the Scottish system, our interviewees only included those outward migrants who, like Andy, had subsequently returned to Scotland. Moreover, qualitative encounters introduce a stronger possibility of interviewer bias, as interviewees inevitably shape and negotiate the interview process in the light of what (and whom) they see in front of them. All of these limitations mean that we should proceed with caution in considering the formation of learning generations in the British context. Nevertheless, it seems to us that the idea of learning generations is an important one in helping to understand what learning means to people and how they approach it through their lives.

## Inter-generational learning

The discussion so far has concentrated on generations as groupings based on age cohort and shared experience. Another body of work looks at inter-generational learning within families (e.g. Gorard et al. 1999; Boström 2003) or the reproduction of educational – and other – inequalities across generations (e.g. Istance 2003). Alison Fuller and colleagues have considered generational differences in higher education access, but with particular respect to inter-generational transmission of inequality, in their

Table 5.1 School reforms and generations in Britain

| Generation | Education as privileged resource | Growing educational opportunity | Welfare and educational choice | Extended schooling, risky transitions | Permanent lifelong education |
|---|---|---|---|---|---|
| Years of birth | 1915–1940 | 1941–1960 | 1961–1970 | 1970–1985 | 1986–???? |
| Entered school | 1920–1944 | 1945–1965 | 1966–1975 | 1976–1990 | 1990–???? |
| School reforms | Universal primary education, wartime disruption of schooling and transition to work; elite higher education | Education Acts 1944/1947; universal secondary education (tripartite in England and Wales but moving towards comprehensive in Scotland); elite higher education; post-war boom and tight labour market | Comprehensive secondary education, above all in Scotland but also in England and Wales; expansion of higher education | Some continued expansion of higher education and growth of early years provision; C&IT is new; disrupted transition from school to work; youth unemployment and growing participation in upper secondary education | Achievement of mass higher education; partial feminisation of higher education; marketisation (strongest in England); C&IT is normal; continuing structural and curricular revolution |
| Age in 2005 | 65–90 | 45–64 | 35–44 | 20–35 | ??–19 |

Source: Adapted from the Finnish model presented in Aro et al. (2005: 463)
C&IT: communications and information technology.

study of barriers to participation in higher education in England (Heath et al. 2007). Gender again plays a central role. Partly this is because primary care responsibilities, whether for children or for the infirm elderly, is far more likely to lie with women than with men.

Ethnicity may similarly play a distinctive role in inter-generational learning. Particularlyamong migrant groups, inter-generational exchanges appear both to help maintain existing collective identities while simultaneously enabling adjustment to a new context. A recent qualitative sociocultural study of child/grandparent learning among Sylheti/ Bengali-speaking families in east London explored the ways in which grandparents served as 'founts of knowledge' that had been passed on in the past, including key social and communicative competences; equally, though, the children brought new competences that older adults had not previously accessed, such as familiarity with new technologies (Kenner et al. 2007). This study also noted the important caring role carried out by many grandparents, in a context where mothers are increasingly engaged directly in the labour market.

Jeannie Taylor's account was unusually positive in its portrait of inter-generational learning. Her mother, an Irish immigrant, had gone back to study at the same high school as Jeannie, then went to a local university, where Jeannie followed a year later after leaving school. Both were living at home.

> Having her there and knowing that she was going through the same thing kinda helped especially when there's two out of the five people in the house trying to get peace and quiet to get studying done, so you tend to win that one, but it did make the household kind of difficult because she was then trying to do full-time education as well as running a house so there was a lot of, everybody needs to chip in.

Jeannie also followed her parents into socialist politics, though all of them dropped out in the late 1990s. In turn, Jeannie was helping with her teenaged stepdaughter, her partner's child by a previous relationship: 'I spent last weekend helping her with her French homework and he helped her with the Maths homework.' She also showed her a CV from work before shredding it, to give her 'some ideas for herself'.

Jeannie, a manager in telephone banking, came from a stable middle class family where education was the norm. Participating in learning was important to her, and she was busily learning to snowboard at the time of our sixth and final interview with her, as well as continuing with a dance class and taking courses at work. She also planned to take a yoga course, and was looking at the possibility of a qualification as a trainer. Jeannie is visibly very confident in her ability to learn, seeing herself both as creative and in control of her life. Her story is very much that of someone belonging to a family habitus that expected to take education seriously, seeing it as a way of getting on and achieving your life goals, and gave one another support and help in learning.

However, inter-generational transmission is not always simple and unilinear. As we have seen, Lui Carter resisted aspects of inter-generational socialisation, refusing the identity of Pakistani migrant in Britain, yet also wishing to retain his status as a full family member and also maintaining his Muslim faith. Lui believed that the reasoning skills he had learned at work, in a large customer relations centre, were helping him balance the conflicting demands of the two worlds:

> quite often what I try and do with myself in my head is try and think of the strategy that I use at work and the type of thinking techniques that I use at work, self-discipline etcetera, and try and apply those to situations outside of work to see if it helps any and think about things, you know, logically.

This did not, though, help Lui with one aspect of his new identity: he had come out to his mother and his ex-wife as a gay man, but was reluctant to discuss his sexuality with any other members of his family. He had decided, he said, that

> You can't, you can't reconcile it I've heard so many people in similar situations that have said that being Asian and not being straight are two things that will never mix because being from an Asian background it's automatically expected of you that you have to marry, not you should, you have to get married... What we're trying to do in my generation is trying to maintain the peace and respect of our parents and understanding, you know, respect of the family and the honour and not bringing on shame, you're torn between that and the life that you're really leading which is living in the western open-minded world where things aren't as suppressed and frowned upon as they are back in India or Pakistan or wherever.

This was, then, a sharp generational clash where Lui had learned to 'understand two sets of rules', which also involved him in learning how 'to lead two different lives'. It is probably not surprising, then, that Lui was pleased rather than dismayed when his employer proposed to relocate the call centre, and him with it, to another town.

## Conclusions

Collective cultural identities may be overlaid with more material foundations of generation, which can entail denial of opportunity to others from older or younger generations. This is made highly visible in current debates about access to housing for those who came of age at a time of rapidly rising prices, who find the housing market dominated by members of older generations. But if we look at education, then it is older generations who are excluded from parts of the labour market that are open to the beneficiaries of the educational expansions of the 1970s through to the 1990s. The expansion of graduate occupations may provide welcome opportunities to those who have been through today's mass higher education system, but it is closed to those who came of age in the period of minority, even elite, higher education.

So the creation of generational identities is partly agentic and partly the outcome of history. This can then include age-based definitions for limiting access to and exclusion from public resources, which are as important in education as in many other areas. These also change over time, sometimes with increasing significance when particular age cohorts appear to pull the drawbridge up as soon as they have crossed it themselves – as, for example, has been the case with recent changes in student funding in higher education. The post-grant-and-fee generation is not only different from the Boomer generation in its experience of higher education – it is likely to resent the way that politicians from Boomer age groups treated those who came afterwards.

Ideas about learning generations can and should inform practice as well as policy. Good teachers already take time to get to know adult students' biographies, and will identify and be sensitive to any difficult earlier experiences of education (Barton et al. 2007: 136–137). These should be understood, though, not simply as private troubles, best left to teachers and others who work directly with the learner, but also as shared, public issues. Further, the potential for inter-generational learning has been underdeveloped. Yet there is some evidence from other fields that inter-generational practice can be beneficial for learning, as well as producing positive effects on well-being and cohesion. While much of this literature focuses on the learning and well-being of children (see the systematic review summarised in Springate et al. 2008), there is also some evidence that inter-generational practices may reduce isolation and raise self-esteem among older people, as well as enabling them to acquire and develop new skills and knowledge (Boström 2003; Kenner et al. 2007). It is therefore important, at least potentially, across the lifecourse and not only in the early years.

Generational relationships and identities can therefore serve as resources for learning, and sometimes as barriers to learning. Generational narratives are often collective, emphasising shared experiences, with common turning points coming to serve as references that mean something similar to others who belong to the same group. Generational attachments are therefore an element in people's positions and dispositions, ideas that are developed further in the next chapter. At this stage we wish to stress that these generational experiences and meanings have consequences for orientations towards learning, as well as for people's dispositions more broadly. Of course, like any other collective basis for identity, they can be something of a burden or constraint, as well as serving as a resource. In addition to helping people develop the skills and understandings that can take them through challenge and change, they can also inhibit and restrict the repertoire of responses that are available. And as we have seen, this is the case for people's dispositions towards learning, as well as for the nature of their involvement in it.

# Chapter 6

# Positions and dispositions

## Introduction

Turning points in people's lives are often a time of learning. These periods of transition frequently involve a change in people's position, whether social, cultural or geographical; and in the conditions and circumstances in which they live. This chapter explores the relationship between learning, positions and the self. We explore this using a number of concepts drawn from the work of Pierre Bourdieu, the French social scientist who is well known for his studies of education and culture (Bourdieu 1984). In these studies, Bourdieu distinguishes between the idea of *position* as a specific social, economic and cultural locus in the social space; and that of *habitus*, which comprises a set of *dispositions*, or propensities towards particular values and behaviours. Our interest, clearly, lies in the relationship between position, disposition and learning.

Earlier research has shown that people's dispositions towards learning can and do change over time, even over relatively short periods (Bloomer and Hodkinson 2000). Yet these changes are not always in a single direction: people's dispositions can change in a variety of ways, and are developed dynamically over time; they may incorporate a degree of hostility to educational institutions and teachers, as well as a growing interest in what education can offer (Crossan et al. 2003).

Adults have widely differing dispositions towards learning. For many learning is merely a factor of life, being seen more as a continual striving to deal with new problems in their lives than as learning per se; for a minority the sense of being a learner is an important part of their identity, and in some cases this learner identity is focused around formal educational provision but always with substantial informal learning related to it; while learning is sometimes valued primarily for the outcomes it brings, people often value the process of engagement in learning for its own sake. It follows that people's judgements about what counts as good or worthwhile learning differ significantly and that the judgements of individuals may be at odds with official policy, which can impact negatively on adults' opportunities to learn what is important to them.

## Positioning

Our findings show that people's positioning tends to influence their learning in three broad and overlapping ways. First, people occupy what might be called positions within a wider social and economic context. All of the stories in this book show the significance of such structural positioning on lives and learning. Of course it is true that these structures are made and remade by people, but their effects are nevertheless felt and narrated as very real. For example, gender, ethnicity and social class are all important and they influence life and learning in complex ways. One way of illustrating this is to imagine that one of these structural factors is suddenly and radically changed: it becomes immediately obvious that one's life, and one's learning, would not be the same as it is now. So although we are not arguing that social structures determine learning, we are clear that learning lives are always structured lives.

Second, position is always historical and geographical. Place is always important in our stories, though often it is taken for granted, at least until someone moves their location. And by the historical dimension, we are noting that each person's narrative is a story of its time. As we showed in Chapter five, the stories of people who belong to a particular generation will often share some similar experiences, as a result of living their lives through a given historical period. Once more, we are not claiming that these dimensions of position invariably determine lives and learning, simply that their influence is ever present. The strength and significance of those influences will vary from person to person, from place to place, and from time to time; they can be more or less significant in different parts of a person's life and learning. In some cases, as we show in Chapter Four, they may be subjected to narrative reflection, and also become resources for narrative learning. However, they can never be completely transcended.

The third way of understanding position in relation to learning is in reference to the places where people learn. There is now an abundant literature on the ways in which learning is rooted in specific webs of social relationships and cultural contexts. Much of this writing has come in response to Jean Lave and Ettienne Wenger's idea of 'situated learning'. As Lave and Wenger put it, learning is not just a cognitive activity taking place inside the brain, but is always also a social practice through which people co-construct knowledge. Further, they claim that 'learning is not merely situated in practice – as if it were some independently reifiable process that just happened to be located somewhere; learning is an integral part of generative social practice in the lived-in world (Lave and Wenger 1991: 35).

Hodkinson et al. (2007) argue that the best way of understanding the contexts in which learning is embedded is as 'learning cultures', defined as the practices through which people learn (see also James and Biesta 2007). This includes any context in which people live, such as their family, local community, leisure or sporting group, workplace, school, faith community, holiday, voluntary activity and so on. All of these can be seen as generating cultural practices that influence learning. It follows that when someone participates in this learning culture it therefore influences their learning, and equally that their involvement in turn (re)shapes the learning culture. And of course, no one ever belongs to one culture only; rather, they are exposed to and participative more or less actively in a number of different learning cultures, some of which may become more or less significant over time.

However, it is not just a matter of which learning cultures a person is part of. What is also important is their position within that culture. This can easily be illustrated in relation to family and employment, though it can hold true for any learning culture. Often this involves relations of power; in the workplace, for example, there is usually a formal hierarchy, and also an informal one, and a person's position within this pecking order will influence his or her learning. There are also hierarchies in the intimate sphere of family relations; we tell below the story of Wafa Jabeen, who spent a critical period of her life in the home of her husband's extended family; we also recount some of Gladys Dean's story as a working class British woman who migrated from the West Indies, and spent much of her mature life caring for her children, and then – it was 'taken for granted' – her children's children. Power relations matter within learning cultures, and are in turn related to positions.

We have presented these three ways of understanding position and learning culture as though they are easily distinguished. In practice, of course, they overlap with one another. One value way of conceptualising these overlaps is through Bourdieu's concept of *field*. A field, for Bourdieu, is 'a network, or configuration, of objective relations between positions' (Bourdieu and Wacquant 1992: 97). Fields are loosely bounded and are structured horizontally as well as vertically. Positions within the field reflect, for Bourdieu, the interplay of people's resources (social capital, cultural capital and economic capital) and their habitus on the one hand, and the rules of the field on the other. Fields can also involve struggles for position between different people and groups.

The concept is thus inherently relational, seeing people in terms of their relations with others rather than as isolated units. People's dispositions and actions, their interactions and inter-subjective ties all contribute to the relations in a field. Further, Bourdieu sees the field not as an external context, but as something to which people are integral, through their positions and dispositions.

Within any learning culture, learning is an integral part of the practices involved in participating in that culture. This may sound tautological at first, but it is not. The nature of any learning culture and its practices will promote some learning, making it more likely, and in some cases enabling reflection on the process of learning itself; but it will also constrain and indeed prevent some learning, making reflection on this undesirable learning less likely. Often these patterns will be taken for granted; someone learning accountancy, for example, is not likely in most circumstances to find out how to defraud their clients, and both they and their fellows will probably give very little thought to this constraint. However, this is a relatively clear-cut example, and exactly what any individual learns in any learning culture depends in part on the position of that individual within the culture, on their approach to the culture, and on their actions within it, always in relation to the many other factors influencing the field, including its own rules and codes (written and unwritten).

Theorising the complex ways in which position influences learning helps us illuminate and understand the many different examples of learning through life. Position influences learning in ways that are multifaceted, non-deterministic and fully cognisant of power relations and inequalities. But what remains to be explored is the impact of people and learning on learning cultures. People are part of learning cultures, and by participating actively in those learning cultures they contribute to their ongoing (re) construction.

## Dispositions, self and identity

If positions and learning cultures both influence learning, then so do individuals. In considering how and why, we find it helpful to think of the person in three different ways: dispositions, the embodied self, and identity. Again, these are overlapping categories, and they change over time. Following Bourdieu, we begin with dispositions.

### Dispositions

Bourdieu says that all of us have a *habitus* – an array of enduring and often tacit dispositions towards every aspect of our life. These dispositions develop through life, and are strongly influenced by a person's position. Bourdieu is mainly interested in the relationship between dispositions and social class. In his work on taste, Bourdieu argues that a particular disposition – in this example, towards a type of music or film – has to be learned. Yet although these competences are closely associated with educational level, he believes they are less likely to be learned consciously, by formal effort, than from the 'unintentional learning made possible by a disposition acquired through domestic or scholastic inculcation of legitimate culture' (Bourdieu 1984: 28), so that their cultural taste is closely related to the social milieu that they inhabit. Our stories confirm this, but they also show that all the other facets of position discussed above can also help to forge a person's dispositions, including their disposition towards learning.

For Bourdieu, dispositions are embodied. People bear their dispositions, and live them, through their bodies: they are emotional, practical and physical (and also cognitive, for the brain, after all, is a body part). They influence all aspects of a person's life, including but not limited to their conscious thoughts. Being embodied, dispositions include a biological aspect, including a psychological dimension, but Bourdieu emphasises that the body must be trained to occupy a habitus and present particular sets of dispositions. Put differently, dispositions are the result of both nature and nurture, but Bourdieu firmly places stress on the importance of nurture.

As noted already, Bourdieu is mainly interested in the interrelations between dispositions and class inequalities. These interrelations are dynamic and transform over time; the dispositions that make up habitus can be changed, and learning is an important mechanism by which dispositions change. In the case of Wafa Jabeen, a change in position – moving to the north of England and living with her husband's extended family while herself becoming a mother – resulted in learning that she described as initially painful but eventually transformative:

> Learning about real life and real relationships and real human nature, that was a big turning point in my life, I think that was the biggest learning so far I have had. Most significant maybe. It affected my life the most and it's actually changed me... I think I'm more able to judge a person by their behaviour than I was before. Or maybe I'm more judgemental, more – I don't know, but it's made me more aware rather than before, I don't know whether I was naive or maybe too trusting but I would always look at the best in people and ignore the bad, if they did anything that was unsuitable or inappropriate I would ignore it... But I've changed my view of that now and I think I'm a bit more cynical now. I always look for double meanings in things.

Wafa was taken aback by much of the 'family politics' that she now experienced; on reflection she recognised that these were largely over issues of control and status, as well as income. When she and her husband bought their own house, she stayed at home to look after her son rather than returning to her job as a primary teacher, later taking a series of courses including Islamic studies and counselling, fitting her learning around her son's schooling.

In some cases, learning may confirm existing dispositions. Jane Eddington was the daughter of an air force pilot who had taken part in the invasion of Italy, a country he came to love; Jane herself had spent part of her childhood in Malta, where her father was then posted, learning some Italian. Her interest in the region was reinforced by a school history course. After leaving school she tried taking a history of art course, but had to leave after failing two subjects, then returned as an adult, only to drop out, subsequently spending six months in Istanbul. After a series of jobs, mainly in office work, and short-lived relationships, as well as several attempts to restart her education, in her mid-fifties Jane was training as a volunteer advocate for people with disabilities. Her enthusiasm for Mediterranean history, culture and languages, however, was undimmed, and throughout her life she has continued to read and learn about the region, and has got to grips with the internet as an additional resource. This intellectual continuity has helped sustain her through numerous life changes and problems. It has motivated her learning, and in turn it has been reinforced by her learning.

It is clear, then, that dispositions influence learning and that learning influence's the nature of a person's dispositions. This is so whether the dispositions change over time or remain largely intact. In practice, though, these two reciprocal influences are not separate, but are continually interwoven with, and constantly influencing, each other. How we orient ourselves towards life and its many possibilities and positions will influence what and how we learn; and our learning in turn directs our orientation towards our lives.

This integral and relational understanding shows a double influence of position on learning. Not only does position directly enable and constrain learning through the nature of learning cultures and the resources available to each person within the learning culture, but it also influences the habitus, which itself enables and constrains learning. This sort of relational thinking is widely supported in the Learning Lives stories, and gives a valuable locker full with conceptual tools to think about the significance of learning in people's lives. This may help us solve the theoretical problem of integrating individual and social (or situational) views of learning (Hodkinson et al. 2008a). However, our interviews also show that thinking of people simply in terms of positions and dispositions is insufficient. We need to consider further aspects of the self, and so we return to the question of the body.

## *The body*

There is an obvious way in which the body is important to learning: our brain undertakes the physical processing of ideas, information and technical skills. But other bodily and mental attributes, including size, strength, demeanour, agility, dexterity and many other attributes influence human activity and therefore learning. A number of men in our study had taken steps towards a career as a professional sports player, usually in football. Stephen Connor, for example, was offered the chance of an apprenticeship with a local professional side as a boy, an opportunity he owed to physical prowess as well as position and disposition. Several other men had been through similar experiences as boys, but none had made it through as a full professional.

Learning often arises from turning points, and these may include changes to the body. We have many examples of situations where people have had to adapt to physical and mental change in similar ways. These sorts of experiences remind us that body and dispositions are not synonymous. However, the body's *role* is not 'purely' physical. Our physical body – including the brain – also needs to be understood in social and cultural terms. Several people told stories of disablement, through illness or accident, or as a result of physical ageing. Derek Hutchinson, a carpenter and joiner with little formal education, had to leave the building industry in his fifties as a result of illness and disability; after a series of part-time jobs, he was working in his sixties as a delivery driver. This process of adaptation to a new body was also a learning process, partly informal and experiential, and partly with professional support, including medical and career guidance.

Bourdieu was interested in the body's relation to habitus. Habitus only exists in and through people and their practices; it therefore is expressed through and formed by embodied actions, including speech, gestures, demeanour and work. He was also interested in the ways that people invested work in the body, learning not merely how to walk or stand or dress or feed, but how to do these things in ways that signalled their membership of a particular class or status group, and reinforced the values and standing of that group (Bourdieu 1984: 190–191). Some of our cases, though, had different concerns. Bourdieu describes the embodied habitus of elite groups, but many of our interviewees, who came from much more modest backgrounds, also saw their bodies as objects of learning.

Many of them talked about periods of depression and anxiety in explicitly physical terms, and some – all female – worried about their body shape. Kathleen Donnelly, for example, told a story of getting 'steaming' (drunk) after her ex-husband called her 'a fat cow'. She also referred to her body shape when booking a holiday abroad.

> Last night I was determined I'm like 'Right I'm gonnae go this holiday and no think oh you're fat, you're ugly, you're this, you're that, get the bikini on and just enjoy yerself 'cause nobody knows you' whereas before when I was younger I seemed to always to focus on my appearance, I don't know, I've suffered from low self-esteem since I was a young lassie, d'you know what I mean.

Consciousness of the body went back a long way for Kathleen. She says that she 'enjoyed primary school, some parts of it but I've got red hair and I was teased since day one'.

In her mid-thirties, Kathleen was taking an Scottish Vocational Qualification 2 (SVQ2) in youth and community work, and working part-time with young people. She was also experimenting with diet and exercise: 'you feel good after you've done a wee bit of exercising and that and still go out walking, trying to get up for my marathon and stuff like that, aye, walking down like big hills and back up them (laughs)'. She was still anxious about her body shape (unnecessarily so in the view of the author who had spoken to her), but had learned to suppress the worst fears while acting to change in a way that would make her more comfortable in her new role.

These stories offer different challenges to the adequacy of understanding learning through the relations between positions and dispositions. Perhaps clumsily, we use the term of the 'embodied self' to supplement and strengthen the analysis. This is because, in different ways, each suggests that there is more to the significance of the self in learning than is captured in the notions of positions and dispositions alone. And ideas of the self are inevitably bound up with the physical reality of the body, and the way we see ourselves inhabiting the body as part of our sense of who we are. This brings us to the concept of identity and its complex relationship with learning.

### *Identity*

Identity is a hotly contested concept, and also one that is confused. It is used in everyday speech, and peppers our interviews. Kathleen Donnelly, for example, was adamant about her own view of position and social standing:

> I don't buy into this where a job makes you, gives you status and makes you the person who you are and I don't buy into the fact that a big fancy bungalow or a house makes me the person who I am, that's not my identity.

While there is a wide-ranging scholarly debate about identity, we have chosen in Learning Lives to adopt a simple definition: we understand it as the way a person sees themselves in the world. Put into Bourdieu's terminology, identity is a matter of a person's dispositions towards and about themselves.

This implies that we see identity as more than just a cognitive concern. People often understand their sense of self in ways that combine the affective (or emotional), the physical and the relational. Much of a person's identity is tacit, or explicit but taken for granted. For example, hardly any of our interviewees talked about their nationality, unless they had experienced movement between different countries, yet we know that national identities often assume considerable importance. When we talk about who we think we are, much is left out – and while this tells us something, not all of the silences are especially significant.

Derek Hutchinson, for example, is eloquent on the significance of where he lives, and about what it means to be a skilled and professional craftsman. He speaks about his family and his pride in his role as a husband, father and grandfather. He rarely talks of being a man, though many of his roles are clearly gendered; he never mentions social class, ethnicity or being British/English. Yet his story, taken as a whole, makes it clear that all of these dimensions are part of his sense of who he is. While we can interpret the interviews to reveal and explore these 'hidden differences', for him they can largely be taken for granted. When asked to narrate their lives and give them a pattern or narrative plot, people foreground the issue of identity, which takes on a more visible and cognitive aspect. Even so, much remains tacit and unstated.

Our data also support those who argue that we have multiple identities. Many people see themselves differently in different situations; as learners, for example, they may be novices in one context and experts in another. Derek Hutchinson talks about himself in the family, at work, and in his hobbies of stamp and postcard collecting. These roles touch on and overlap with each other. So within the family, he presents himself as someone who can help his adult children sort out practical building problems, while in his hobbies and working life he tells of a drive for perfection through attention to detail. So these dimensions are not discrete, but neither are they to be found in a unified, single, essential 'true self'. Our data also show that even for one person, some identities change while others remain the same.

Identity is related to habitus; but it is both more and less than habitus. It is less because we all have dispositions towards a wide range of things, not just towards our self; and it is more in so far as our sense of who we are permeates and underpins many of our dispositions towards our life and the world. Like dispositions, identity is shaped by one's position, and indeed can only be understood in relation to the different types of position we hold through life. As our positions change, this may alter some existing identities while reinforcing others. And this also holds true in respect of learning.

The relations between position, disposition, identity and learning are inevitably complex. Our data make it clear that at any point in time and in any specific space, the nature of the self strongly influences our learning. What and how a person learns are enabled and constrained by who they think they are and might become in the world – that is, by their identity. Put differently, the nature of the self places boundaries around what learning is possible or might become possible, and therefore influences the likelihood of some learning rather than other learning within those boundaries. Yet there can often be tensions or even contradictions between and within dispositions and identity, and both can be in tension with other aspects of the self, such as bodily health.

Of course the various dimensions of the self are not static. Rather, they are best understood as a mixture of continuity and change. When we argue that the nature of the self enables and constrains learning, we are concerned with a dynamic self, with a given history and with a potential for change.

In our stories, the ways in which learning contributes to disposition and position is most apparent at turning points. These are significant moments of personal change, which tend to foreground issues of identity for the person. The most charged turning points may help promote reflexivity about identity that then provide a basis for what we have described as narrative learning. They are therefore extremely important in our account of position, disposition and identity in prompting or constraining learning.

At risk of oversimplifying, we can identify three broad types of relationship between learning and the self in turning points. These are:

1   Learning can facilitate positive changes in disposition and identity. For Gladys Dean, this happened after she enrolled on a literacy course. Taking the course contributed to changes in her disposition towards her life, and especially towards her self, and while some of her identities have remained unchanged, others have been transformed.

2   Learning can result from tensions and conflicts arising from a change. In Wafa Jabeen's case, the main tensions arose between her sense of herself as an independent Muslim woman, and her position within her husband's family. There were also further tensions between different aspects of her dispositions, for example between the Wafa who enjoyed her professional standing and career, and the Wafa who wanted to be a mother and carer for her children. Learning played a part in her adjustment, involving some changes in her dispositions and identity. In this, she also drew on her economic capital (to buy a house) and cultural capital (she knew her way around the education system) to join and succeed in the educational activities that helped transform her life.

3   Learning can be involved in situations where no satisfactory resolution is achieved. Sergei Seminov's failed asylum application left him in such a position. He found it difficult to reconcile his legal position with his dispositions towards a new identity; now he was not Russian, could not be Estonian and had been turned away by Britain. Others found themselves stuck within their learning. Kathleen Donnelly felt manipulated by the Scottish Vocational Qualification (SVQ) system, which, she believes, allows professionals working in community development to advance their own interests,

and it's annoying me because when we started on this project it was all full of this great ethos where "You'll go out and do good for the community, it's people like you that are needed, you'll get a qualification, we've got 100 per cent success rate in jobs and stuff". I have wrote sixteen or seventeen job applications and CV's out and not one company has said "Sorry you've been unsuccessful", not one of them and I think it's a bunch of lies, I think the whole thing's a bunch of lies, but I don't know how to protest about it'.

She reports feelings of immobility and does not see how she can live a different and more fulfilled life.

These examples show that the relationships between learning and changing identities and dispositions are complex, and not always positive. People are in different positions and can access different levels of resources (capitals) to pursue their goals. And learning can either cause change (as in Gladys's case) or occur as a result of change (as in Wafa's case).

An important role in this is played by the person's *horizons for learning*. People's possibilities for learning are bounded, though these horizons are neither fixed nor sharply demarcated. They depend partly on the person's position, influenced by the nature of the learning culture in which the person participates, and the health, dispositions, identity and resources of the person. This brings us to the question of agency, by which we mean the extent to which people are able to control their own lives, and feel themselves in control of their lives (see Biesta and Tedder 2007).

## Agency and learning

Agency is always situated in a given context, temporal as well as spatial. It is not a quality of individuals, whereby a given person is 'agentic' or not, but rather a quality of engagement with context. As Biesta and Tedder (2007) put it, we require an ecological understanding of agency, which is achieved through engagement with context, and represents an ability to change one's positions and dispositions. Such processes are often tacit, happening as much within what Giddens (1991) terms practical consciousness as in discursive consciousness. This may involve making changes, but it may also involve people in actions designed to preserve and reinforce existing circumstances, rather than drifting passively with the tide of events. So agency can be important at times of routine, as well as in turning points.

We can illustrate and elaborate these propositions with four exemplar illustrations of the relations between learning and agency. These involve (a) learning and agency in sustaining existing conditions; (b) learning and agency related to identity change; (c) learning and identity related to positional change; and (d) learning and restricted agency. Of course, there are other possible permutations, but these seem to us the most significant.

## Sustaining what exists

Jane Eddington has spent much of her adult life maintaining and reinforcing her existing dispositions towards Mediterranean history, the arts, languages, learning and her sense of self. She has done this through a life of changing material and social circumstances, including some periods of hardship and some serious personal setbacks. Her identity, agency and learning are reciprocally reinforcing her sense of who she is and what matters in her life. However, her agency and identity are also shaped by other factors in her life, including the meaning she attributes to relationships.

William Moore was agentic in relation to his identity as a working male. As his textile design business declined, he worked hard initially to sustain the business, and then to develop an alternative career. Formal career guidance helped him identify new jobs that he might achieve, and he also learned how to set about obtaining a new job, finding work in a music shop. Of equal importance in this instance was his earlier learning to play music, which in turn was part of his established identity as a music lover. Serendipity also played a part, in that the vacancy occurred at a time when he was seeking work. Though William used learning to sustain part of his identity, as a working male, it led to an important identity shift as he found that he enjoyed working for an organisation without the pressures of being the boss.

## Identity change

Gladys Dean would never have enrolled in a literacy course without two external factors. One was the availability of a suitable class in her area, as part of a government initiative to counter illiteracy. The second was pressure from her daughter, who applied for a place in the class and pressed her to attend. So her decision to join the course involved limited agency on Gladys's part, but once on board her learning brought significant dispositional changes. She speaks of becoming much more confident in everyday encounters involving reading and writing, and this slowly became a more general confidence. Ironically, it even gave her the resilience to stand up to her daughters. In Emirbayer and Mische's (1998) terms, she was able to move beyond her past, radically altering her present and envisaging a different future. This involved mutually reinforcing changes in identity and learning as well as agency.

## Positional change

Wafa Jabeen made a direct positional change when moving in with her parents-in-law, but it arose from her husband's decision rather than her own. Although she had been highly agentic in her previous situation, she struggled to assert her own values and interests in this new environment, where she had less social and cultural capital, finding herself in a position of relative weakness. When she and her husband moved out into a house of their own, the possibilities for agentic action expanded, and Wafa took control over her life while embracing a new identity as a non-working mother, caring for others while taking a number of educational courses to sustain her independent and rather academic earlier identity.

### *Restricted agency*

Willie Cotter, a working class Glaswegian, has experienced long-term unemployment, and has attended a range of short- and long-term courses designed to enable a move into employment. Willie finds these very interesting but says that they are only 'educational'; they appear to be irrelevant to how he lives his life. He cannot describe the future. He imagines an impossible future, one where his son is still alive, his daughter does not abuse heroin and he can look forward to grandchildren. As he believes in none of these he makes do with passing time absorbed in movies and drawing pictures. While he has been an active community member, and was again at the time of our last interview, these are sporadic commitments, mostly he claims due to alcohol addiction and intermittent binge drinking.

Willie recounts his life as a story narrated by fate. His drinking, he says, is a family trait: 'it was in our family genes, so'. Although enjoying adult education, he saw it as a process of repetition. After completing one course, called 'Goals', he concluded that 'it was a motivation course, it was like your confidence, your self-esteem, blah, blah, blah, for you to be the person that you want to be, do you know that kind of thing'. As for setting himself motivational goals,

> I didn't need anything, just to educate myself, I've no goals, my goals is Wednesday and Saturday, know, the football or the lottery, because that would change it, that would give you goals all right, no, it was just more education for me, more learning, you know.

Far from challenging his low sense of self-worth and limited control over his life, participating in learning has given Willie a way of spending time with others in a similar situation, reinforcing his fatalism and sense of helplessness.

## Conclusions

We have found that dispositions together with positions (such as family, community work) can both enable and constrain learning. Many aspects of the sense of self remain implicit but can become more explicit at times of change and crisis, although this is not necessarily the case as particular dispositions and a particular sense of self may also prevent learning and change. The narration of one's life story is not only an important vehicle for expressing one's sense of self, but also for articulating and actively constructing such a sense of self. Relationships between identity and learning often become clear at times of crisis and change. When people go through major life-changing epiphanies or turning points, they are often presented by a need to learn. Learning can then contribute to changes in some dispositions, and thus a person's identity. It is, however, possible that existing dispositions are so strong that learning and subsequent change in identity do not happen. Our data suggest a widespread 'need' for the construction of a (coherent) life story that helps them to make sense and come to terms with their life, although we also have clear evidence of the situated nature of life stories (that they are told and constructed for particular purposes and in particular social settings), and that people often maintain a distinction between a private and a public version of their life story.

# Part 3

# What are the overall implications?

# Chapter 7

# Improving learning through the lifecourse

In the preceding chapters we have provided an overview of the main insights and findings from the Learning Lives project. Given the complex and multifaceted nature of the project and also given its sheer size and scope we have not been able to provide much detail. In this respect this book should indeed be read as a gateway into further project publications. For similar reasons we will not attempt in this final chapter to bring all insights generated through the project together in one set of encompassing conclusions. Rather, our ambition in this chapter is to indicate some of the main implications from our research for the improvement of learning through the lifecourse. In particular, we consider the enhancement of dispositions, learning practices, attainments and opportunities for people to use their skills and knowledge to assert control over their lives.

## The value of learning in people's lives

Our research covered both formal and informal learning. What is often termed informal learning is a ubiquitous part of living. Such informal learning arises mainly out of the experiences of living. It can be significant or insignificant, intended or unintended, and transformative or trivial. Much is often tacit and unrecognised as learning, even by those concerned. In addition, many people participate in formal learning, not just in childhood and youth but across the lifespan. Such participation in formal learning varies along a continuum between low and high involvement, depending upon the extent to which the process of learning itself becomes important in the life and sense of self of the person.

The question of involvement is an important one. For us, it means going beyond what is often implied by terms such as participation or engagement. People can engage in learning, yet feel that it is peripheral to what really matters in their lives, or marginal to their sense of who they really see themselves as being. Alternatively, they can value learning as an integral part of their lives, and see it as central to who they are.

Our research confirms other studies in showing that most adult participation in formal learning is related to work. We have further found that much work-related training elicits low levels of involvement. Participation in more general adult education frequently results in high levels of involvement and is often, but not always, triggered by significant life-changing events. Our research also shows that people learn from reflecting upon and thinking about their lives, often but not exclusively triggered by life-changing events.

It is not possible to make evaluative judgements about strategies for improving lifelong learning, without first making normative judgements about what king of learning is of value. In particular, our research shows that not all learning is beneficial, and that what counts as valuable learning can differ according to point of view. For example, there are often differences between the value placed upon learning in government policy, and what many people see as valuable in their lives. In general terms, our research shows that people can experience learning as valuable in the following circumstances:

- Learning can help people with the processes of routine living.
- Learning can help people adjust to changed circumstances.
- Learning can provide valuable knowledge or skills for particular purposes, which can include employment and career change, as well as other activities – which may or may not influence their experiences in the labour market.
- Learning can contribute to the development of one's sense of self.
- Learning can contribute to the achievement of agency.

However, learning for any person or group is always enabled and constrained by their horizons for learning. By that we mean the interrelationships between the person and their situation. This means that there are always limits on what can be learned, so that strategies for improving learning need to vary to meet differing people's needs and different circumstances.

## Strategies for improving learning through the lifecourse

It is important to be pragmatic about what counts as a 'learning strategy'. A working definition is that a strategy for learning involves a planned, coherent approach to providing and/or achieving learning. Such strategies can originate from different types of actor, such as individual adults; those who teach and advise adults; governments, through their policies and funding approaches; and local and regional organisations in the voluntary, private (including employers and trades unions) and public sectors.

The work done within the Learning Lives project suggests four broad approaches to improving learning. They are:

1 Provision of planned courses, workshops etc. ('formal' education and training).
2 Personal support for the learner, which may be professional (career guidance, workplace mentoring, tutoring, provision of learning materials, etc.) or informal (friends, colleagues, family, local community).
3 Enhancing learning cultures, that is, improving opportunities for learning in particular locations (workplace, local community, etc.).
4 Providing opportunities for self-reflection, including talking, writing, thinking about our own life histories and life circumstances.

These often can and should overlap. Each of these approaches works best when it addresses both aspects of a person's horizons for learning: the internal and the external. It is possible to develop strategies for the improvement using any one of these approaches taken independently, and we consider that next. However, there is often more to be gained by looking at them in combination.

## Formal education and training

We have gathered considerable evidence of the value of formal education and training. Where it is of value, formal education has two overlapping types of outcome. The first is the learning of whatever the course was designed to teach. The second is a contribution to personal growth and/ or change. Where adults have a low level of involvement, the emphasis is on the former. Where there is a high level of involvement, the former can become a part of the latter. Then, the process of learning is often at least as important as what is being learned. We have several cases that show that participation in adult education can lead to high levels of involvement. Such high involvers often take several different courses, over several years. Such periods of participation are often linked to significant life-changing events. However, in some cases, participation in adult education continues periodically throughout the person's life.

On the other hand, many in our sample routinely attended short courses or training events that seemed to have no discernable impact upon their identities. Often, these are courses provided by employers, which people can see as relevant to their work, but that do not seem to touch them beyond this instrumental purpose. Such course can also be undertaken voluntarily, usually for a particular purpose – like improving skills with a computer. Our analysis of BHPS data shows that most participation in formal learning is related to employment, and much is therefore likely to be of the low involvement type.

It is, however, not the nature of provision that determines the level of involvement, but the interrelationship between that provision, the individual and the broader positions within which the learning takes place. High levels of involvement do require lengthy periods of participation in one or more courses, so is less likely in circumstances where this is not possible. Where the outcomes of formal learning are only concerned with the acquisition of course content, this is not a problem. But when the hope or intention is to make a difference to or to change the individual, short courses alone are unlikely to be successful. For significant personal change there is a need for longer-term formal provision that can encourage higher levels of involvement, and/or short courses need to be integrated into related informal learning in the individual's life (see below). This finding points up a contradiction in current UK policies towards lifelong learning, which set out ambitious goals of personal change for such provision, mainly associated with gaining employment, but also with increasing social inclusion, whilst focusing primarily on short course provision (for example through learndirect), and on the acquisition of specified content outcomes, measured by qualification achievement. The government has set itself ambitious targets for greater employment and social inclusion, while promoting flexibility and upskilling for all. These objectives must entail significant changes in the sense of self for many of those people whose life chances the government is hoping to improve. Our research suggests that such personal change is least likely to be achieved through short courses.

We have found that the value of any formal learning does not depend primarily on the achievement of a qualification (though our evidence includes plenty of cases where this has been valuable and even essential for some people). Many, perhaps most adults, take formal learning provision aimed at a level the same as or below their previous best qualifications. So successful formal learning for adults does not depend on climbing a linear hierarchy of qualifications. A final point is that some groups have specific needs, and these will require targeted provision. Many of these groups are already well-known from previous studies, but some are less familiar. Our analysis of BHPS data, for example, showed that a number of groups who are not in the workforce are missing out. This includes young women who had early transitions into parenthood, and as some of this group showed a preference for learning at home, they may benefit from access to targeted and supported online provision. The BHPS analysis also indicated that older adults (54+) do not seem to be catered for at all in the present skills drive.

We also have evidence of formal education and training that had negative effects on people. A lot of the negative experience relates to early schooling, but not all. Some derives from participation in formal learning in adult life, which for one reason or another is experienced not only as unsatisfactory in some way but, more fundamentally, serving to 'switch off' motivation for any further formal participation. Disturbingly, this included instances where adults were highly frustrated by their experience of working towards a vocational qualification.

Our research shows that many adults live successful and fulfilled lives without much participation in formal learning. However, it also shows that many people gain considerably from such engagement. Our research further suggests that current strategies and provision of formal learning in the UK have some serious shortcomings. These include:

- An excessive focus on learning related to employment.
- A lack of accessible provision for people who are not in employment.
- A lack of longer provision that is likely to sustain personal growth through high levels of involvement.
- An over-focus on content acquisition as demonstrated by qualification achievement.
- Particularly in England, a dangerous restriction of funding to hierarchical qualification improvement.

These shortcomings can be overcome, and if the intention is to build a learning society for all, their negative impact should be removed.

## Personal support

We have lots of data suggesting the importance of personal support in improving learning. This can happen within formal courses, and also in relation to wide ranges of more informal or everyday learning. The support can be from one individual or from a supportive group. It can be professional – career guidance, workplace mentoring or a tutor on a formal course. It can also be provided through informal contacts, with relatives, friends, work colleagues, local community groups or classmates, for example.

Strategies for improving professional personal support in learning can be thought of in three ways. First, all formal learning provision contains an element of personal support, from a tutor or teacher. In addition, some courses also involve further support, for example from a mentor. In either case, this personal support role can be very important. Second, many workplaces provide professional support for individuals (perhaps especially new staff). This can be through an official mentor or, more informally, though the day-to-day guidance from more experienced colleagues. Third, there are professional agencies, both government funded and within the voluntary sector, who provide personal support in relation to particular types of situation. Examples include marriage guidance, debt avoidance, psychotherapy and career guidance. At the heart of all these activities is the learning of the client, usually about themselves in relation to a major personal change or crisis. Our research contains several examples where such support has been very valuable, and suggests that recent attacks on a supposedly growing therapeutic culture are overstated.

Personal support for learning works best when the person giving the support can focus on the wants and interests of the client. Attempts to push people into doing things they do not want to do, and the rationale for which they do not accept, often result in avoidance, resistance or strategic compliance. Such learning support also works best when the support and learning are interrelated with other activities and learning in the person's life. A serious strategic concern is the very uneven access to such professional learning support, beyond formal learning provision. This is partly a matter of availability, partly a matter of cost and partly a matter of personal awareness of what such support services can offer, and what the benefits can be.

Non-professional support takes place through the family, friendships and communities within which people live. It can be usefully seen as part of social capital. Our research includes people who have successfully built social networks to help support their learning, and even examples of people who have cut themselves off from what they regarded as inhibiting ties. It follows that such support is best improved through activities directed at improving social networking, and the availability of personal support in a general sense. It also suggests that co-presence can be an important resource for learners, particularly those most at risk of disengagement from learning programmes. We argue below that this is one part of a strategy for enhancing learning cultures.

### Enhancing learning cultures

A major limitation on the learning of some people is the impoverishment of the learning cultures with which they engage. Any social situation has a learning culture, by which we mean the practices through which people learn in that situation. Such situations include the family, the local community, workplaces, education institutions and leisure or voluntary pursuits. The enhancement of a person's learning cultures can be approached in two ways. First, the learning culture of any specific situation can be enhanced. Second, people can be given access to a greater range of situations where learning takes place.

Within any particular situation, the learning culture can be enhanced in ways that make valuable learning more likely. This can be done through expanding the range of challenges and opportunities within the situation, thus broadening the learning practices that a person can participate in. For example, work can be organised to create new challenges and opportunities, or line managers can adopt an enthusiastic and proactive approach to learning rather than a sceptical and obstructive stance. A sports club might offer chances to become involved in management, as well as playing. Another way to enhance a specific learning culture is to increase the opportunities for shared and collaborative activity, where participants can learn from each other. This is particularly important in the light of developments in technology-enhanced learning, which may need to be used in conjunction with co-presence.

Furthermore, research shows that learning is more likely to be effective if the many forces acting upon a learning culture are acting synergistically with the learning concerned. For example, members of a sports club are more likely to learn cooperation and team work if (1) the game being played requires such cooperation to bring success; (2) the influential members of the club are themselves exemplars of cooperation; (3) distinction within the club is earned at least partly through such cooperation; and (4) the learners want to become better team players. This is one example, and similar considerations apply in other organisational settings, such as workplaces.

The learning cultures of different situations differ considerably, even when two situations have the same purpose. It follows that detailed attempts to improve the learning culture of any situation must be situation specific. Furthermore, in most situations, learning is not the prime function. Workplaces, to take an obvious example, exist primarily to produce a particular product or service. It follows that any enhancement of the learning culture will normally be secondary to the achievement of that prime function. And, of course, attempts to shape cultures can go badly wrong if they are not carefully thought through. Enhancing the learning culture in any situation therefore has to be pragmatic. Nevertheless, this particular approach to improving learning is currently neglected, and much more could be done.

Many successful adults already live in a range of situations that combine to provide rich learning cultural variations. However, an important way of understanding the problems faced by the least advantaged sectors of society is that they lack access to this rich variety, in ways that severely limit their learning. We can give two examples from the Learning Lives data. First, when people are not employed, one major situation where learning is possible is removed. The unemployed and the retired not only have reduced access to formal learning, they lack participation in the learning culture of work. Second, some people live in deprived areas. Most policy and research focuses on issues of poverty, unemployment and health in defining and analysing such communities. However, they are also areas with relatively few accessible situations that provide rich learning cultures. Indeed, such areas are often stigmatised by outsiders in ways that further inhibit attempts to broaden social networks and promote reliance on limited internal resources.

One way of improving learning in such disadvantaged and stigmatised communities is to expand and sustain opportunities for both informal and formal learning within them. For example, a stable local learning centre and/or sports provision can valuably enhance the culture of a rundown inner city area, or isolated rural community. Formal learning centres in such deprived areas should be seen as an ongoing learning resource, not just a means to access courses for instrumental reasons, and certainly not as a temporary measure tied to a particular funding programme or regeneration initiative.

### Personal reflection and narrative learning

The project has generated extensive evidence of biographical learning, that is to say, of ways in which adults learn *from* their lives. The life-history methodology has helped us to explore the significance of narrative and narration in such learning processes, something we have captured in the idea of 'narrative learning'. The idea of 'narrative learning' has been clarified through the course of this study. Stories and storying are important vehicles for learning from one's life, and our evidence shows how differences in the 'narrative quality' of life stories (i.e. narrative intensity; descriptive–evaluative quality; plot and emplotment; flexibility of storying) are correlated with different learning processes (the 'learning potential' of life stories) and differing learning outcomes (the 'action potential'). There are important differences in the efficacy of life storying and there appear to be important relationships between styles of narration, forms of narrative learning and agency. Life stories play a crucial role in the articulation of a sense of self, which means that narrative learning is also a form of 'identity work'.

We have taken agency to be about the (situated) ability to give direction to one's life. We have found that learning itself may or may not be agentically driven: it can be self-initiated or forced by others or be incidental. Learning may result in increase or decrease of agency. Increased agency seems to be more obvious and common, but much depends on the extent to which people acknowledge that they have learned something. This is more obvious in relation to formal education, often because qualifications open up new possibilities for action. Yet, experiences of successful learning also impact positively on people's self-confidence, which in turn can lead to increased agency in many aspects of their lives. The research indicates that the extent to which learning 'translates' into agency depends on a range of factors and also on the particular 'ecological' conditions of people's field of action. Decreased agency through learning occurs when people learn that things are too difficult or that they cannot cope, which, in turn, impacts upon their sense of self.

The narration of one's life story is not only an important vehicle for expressing one's sense of self, but also for articulating and actively constructing such a sense of self. Relationships between identity and learning often become clear at times of crisis and change. People's major, life-changing turning points often involve a need to learn. Learning can then contribute to changes in some dispositions, and thus a person's identity. It is, however, possible that existing dispositions are so strong that learning and subsequent change in identity do not happen. Our data suggest a widespread 'need' for the construction of a (coherent) life story that helps them to make sense and come to terms with their life, although we also have clear evidence of the situated nature of life stories (that they are told and constructed for particular purposes and in particular social settings), and that people often maintain a distinction between a private and a public version of their life story.

The 'capability' of learning from one's life is not fixed but can change over time. We have found that narrative learning operates at the intersection of 'internal conversations' and social practices of storytelling, which means that for many the (social) opportunities for narrating one's life story are an important vehicle for narrative learning. Our work is therefore consistent with other studies that emphasise the importance of a 'social practice pedagogy', ensuring that learners can contribute their own experiences, grasping the distinctiveness of each learner's life narrative and establishing common ground where different people's narratives can be heard and valued.

## Combining the approaches

Often, a successful strategy for improving learning will combine some or all of these four approaches. We show how this might work by taking three examples.

### *Learning at work*

Other research, in addition to ours, shows that the most important factor influencing learning at work is the nature of work itself (Felstead et al. 2009). That is, employers or trades unions who wish to improve learning at work should first focus upon what we have termed the learning culture of the workplace. Enhancing this culture might, for example, include providing greater challenges and new work opportunities, increasing cooperative and collaborative working, and modifying working practices that inhibit desired learning. In addition, personal support may be provided through official or unofficial mentoring, and formal courses can also be provided. However, a central problem with learning at work is the tendency to focus only on what the employer values. Where that happens, even the best learning strategies can be counterproductive, from the perspective of the individual worker. For example, mentoring schemes focused too tightly on employer objectives often generate resistance and strategic compliance. In such an environment, helping learners make sense of their own lives may feel more like increased surveillance than empowerment. Equally, well-managed and focused mentoring schemes can help learners broaden their social capital and provide support for informal as well as formal learning.

### Learning at college

Currently, most efforts aimed at improving learning at college focus on teaching, and on how teachers can better relate to their students and help them master the specified curriculum content. Sometimes this is seen as including giving personal support. However, other research suggests that much could be done to enhance the learning cultures in colleges and college classes. Teachers can do some of this. They lack control over the learning cultures in their classrooms, but can mediate those cultures, working on aspects of the cultural practices to make more likely the learning that they wish to promote. Others in the educational system can also do more to enhance college learning cultures – or at least to avoid doing them further damage. College managers, government policy makers and several influential quangos could all do more, if they took the learning cultures issue more seriously. Particularly in adult education, there are examples of teachers explicitly working with students to develop personal narratives, to further enhance their growth and development.

### Community learning

Strategies to improve learning in deprived, stigmatised communities would also benefit from a mixed approach. As we have already argued, the learning culture can be enhanced and formal learning provided. Additional personal support and opportunities for some to reflect upon their lives can also be provided. As Veronica McGivney and others have argued, outreach activities are critical aspects of this process (McGivney 2006); yet learning that is limited to the safe and known settings of a specific workplace or neighbourhood is unlikely to expose learners to the range of skills and knowledge they require in contemporary society.

## Limitations of any strategy

While the Learning Lives research shows that all of these ways of improving learning can work and be beneficial for some people, it also reminds us of vast variations in individual identities and circumstances. No single approach is likely to work for all people all of the time. And, whatever mix of approaches is adopted, there remain central and contested questions about the significance, value and desirability of learning. It is also important to remember that most informal learning is unintentional. This means that when attempts are made to promote particular learning processes and outcomes, there are likely to be additional unforeseen and unintended processes and outcomes, which may sometimes be more powerful than those intended. It is for these reasons that the Learning Lives project endorses approaches from other TLRP research on lifelong learning, in arguing that successful strategies to improve learning are likely to focus on increasing the likelihood of desirable learning in any particular situation, rather than prescribing what should be learned and how.

# Methodological appendix

## Introduction

In the Learning Lives project we combined life-history research with two different forms of lifecourse research: longitudinal interpretative lifecourse research and quantitative survey research. The first two approaches used interviews for data collection. For the second approach we analysed data from the British Household Panel Survey (BHPS), an annual panel survey of each adult member of a nationally representative sample of 5,500 British households (about 10,000 individuals per wave).

## Interviews

Over a period of 36 months we conducted 528 interviews with 117 people, 59 male and 58 female, aged between 25 and 84 at first interview (Figure A.1).

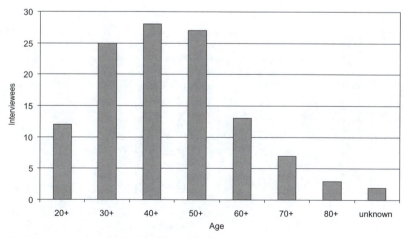

*Figure A.1* Age distribution of interviewees

Most interviews lasted for about two hours. The average number of interviews per individual was four to five; in a small number of cases we conducted up to nine interviews (Figure A.2).

In the interviews we focused initially on the life history by asking participants the question, 'Can you tell me about your life?' Subsequent interviews increasingly focused on ongoing events in the lives of participants. Interviewers took an open approach, asking for clarification and elaboration, with progressive focusing on key project interests and themes. In the final interview participants were asked about their experiences of taking part in the project. All interviews were recorded, transcribed and checked by the interviewer. Transcripts were made available to the participants but they were not required to read or check them.

Building on our experience with the analysis of large qualitative data sets (Hodkinson et al. 2005; James and Biesta 2007), we developed an approach that suited the logistics and objectives of the project. After each interview research fellows wrote short papers, capturing salient experiences and early interpretations. Over time these developed into substantive records of ongoing analysis. We used two approaches for systematic data analysis in an iterative relationship. *Thematic analysis* focused on larger numbers of cases around particular themes, using both theoretically driven analysis and data-driven analysis. *Biographical analysis* focused on the in-depth analysis of individuals and resulted in the construction of detailed individual case studies. Interim findings were reported in conference papers and project working papers; summative analysis was documented in three summative working papers on learning from life, learning through life, and learning and generations. All working papers were made available on

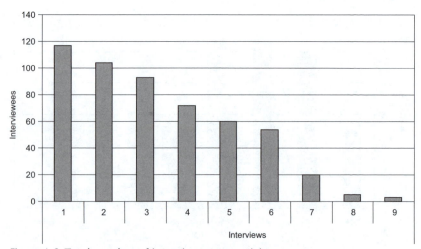

*Figure A.2* Total number of interviews per participant

the project website (www.learninglives.org). Full transcripts of interviews with 55 participants were deposited in order to make data available for other researchers.

## The British Household Panel Survey (BHPS)

The quantitative part of the project was based on an analysis of data derived from the British Household Panel Survey (BHPS), which was designed as an annual survey of each adult (sixteen+) member of a nationally representative random sample of 5,500 households giving a total of approximately 10,000 individuals. These same individuals are being followed over time and re-interviewed in successive annual waves. Fifteen waves of interviews were available to (and used in) the project. Full details about the BHPS can be found on the relevant website (Institute for Social and Economic Research 2010).

The size of the data set, and its long-term nature, gave the project considerable statistical power. In terms of our four key concepts – learning, agency, identity and change – the main advantages of the BHPS were:

1 Lifecourse: the longitudinal structure of the data, the representativeness of the sample covering the full adult age span and the richness of information held about each member collected retrospectively (life history) and in 'real time' (fifteen successive annual waves) concerning the patterns and forces that shaped their lives provided a powerful and authoritative basis for establishing an iterative relationship with our case studies;.

## Learning Lives Summative Working Papers

(available from www.learninglives.org)

Hodkinson, P., with Hodkinson, H., Hawthorn, R. and Ford, G. (2008). Learning through life. Learning Lives Summative Working Paper 1.

Biesta, G.J.J., Goodson, I.F., Tedder, M.T. and Adair, N.A. (2008). Learning from life: The role of narrative. Learning Lives Summative Working Paper 2.

Field, J., Lynch, H. and Malcolm, I. (2008). Generations, the life course and lifelong learning. Learning Lives Summative Working Paper 3.

2 Learning: detailed information on all learning in terms of formal educational and training spells undertaken in the past, their outcomes in terms of qualifications obtained and the annual updating of recent formal learning activities by recording all courses attended and qualifications obtained since September of the year before.

3 Identity: the sample design allowed us to study individuals as members of households, most of which were made up of family groups; major subsections of the UK population were represented; and there were questions on how individuals subjectively positioned themselves on indicators such as health, well-being, social class and disability;.

4 Agency: a validated scale of subjective well-being (CASP-19) was applied in waves 11 and 16, allowing us to focus on responses to questions about two of the four domains that were concerned with autonomy and self-actualisation (Hyde et al. 2003), providing us with a framework for developing and validating longitudinally an individual agency scale using BHPS measures. A scale to measure individual agency using variables from across all waves is being developed and the (forthcoming) wave 16 (2006) data release will provide an important opportunity to validate this instrument as it contains key variables for this process that appear only at waves 11 and 16. This work is being undertaken by an ESRC scholarship PhD student (Ian Alcock, 2006–2009) supervised by Flora Macleod.

The disadvantages of using the BHPS were:

1 Learning: it is weak on measuring the informal and the tacit, but this problem was unlikely to be improved by designing our own instrument; some double counting of participation spells and educational attainments is possible as, due to a design issue, some people may report the same spell and qualification two years running. We have reported this to the BHPS organisers and it is hoped that improvements will be made for subsequent waves.

2 Identity: due to their relative proportions within the UK population, only composite ethnic minority groupings are possible. Even with such a large-scale survey, there are too few cases of each ethnic group to make safe comparisons and estimates of trends.

3 Agency: longitudinal validation of our measure of individual agency is dependent on wave 16, and the data release was still pending when our fieldwork ended, so this work could not be completed within the project's timescale.

# BHPS data analysis

Five different analyses were conducted:

1 patterns and trends in part-time formal education in the UK in relation to nation, class, place, gender, age and disability (1998–2003) using chi-square tests and linear models;
2 predicting the occurrence and timing of transition into adult education amongst 1997 school leavers using event history models;
3 dynamics (stocks and flows) of participation (1992–2005);
4 mapping trajectories of participation in education and training in relation to other lifecourse events (1992–2005) using two-stage latent class models;
5 outcomes of education and training in terms of qualifications across all fifteen waves amongst all those who provided this information.

## *Dependent variables*

In waves 8 to 15 our dependent variable TRAIN came from one item (question): 'Apart from the full time education you have already told me about, have you taken part in any other training schemes or courses at all since September 1st (the previous year) or completed a course or training which led to a qualification?' Interviewers were instructed to include part-time college or university courses, evening classes, training provided by an employer either on or off the job, government training schemes, Open University courses, correspondence courses and work experience schemes, but exclude leisure courses. Interviewers were also instructed to include continuing courses started before September 1st the previous year. Those who answered 'yes' were asked a number of additional 'routed' questions. These included giving a detailed breakdown of the training schemes or courses they had attended during the year including any that were ongoing but excluding any full-time courses that had been asked about earlier in the interview. They were also asked where the course or training took place and whether each course had led to a qualification, part qualification or no qualification.

## *Development of a derived variable for participation (1991–1997)*

As there was no comparable variable to TRAIN for this period we had to develop one. First we separated out those in full-time education from those participating part-time. JBSTAT (Current Economic Activity – interviewees invited to self-describe) and NEMST (Current Labour Force Status – imposed categories) were used to identify those who self-describe as being in full-time education and to get at other variables relevant to participation that were routed through them. Because one of these variables allows self-description and the other does not there is potential for two different responses from the same person. Although consistency was high we found marginal differences. For example, someone in paid work at the time immediately prior to the interview, such as the previous week, who is generally unemployed may self-describe as being 'in work' but not when given the option of choosing between the categories 'employed'/'unemployed'.

We adopted a pragmatic approach to identifying cases engaged in full-time educational activity through the self-description variables by identifying cases self-classifying as either 'full-time student / at school' or 'on a government training scheme'. However, the deeper problem of people's self-descriptions being more tied to 'the period immediately prior to the day of the interview' as opposed to their more usual status during that whole year remained. This was resolved by using the job status history spells routed through the variable NEMST. This gave more substantive facts about activities during the whole wave period. We thus used a derived variable similar to TRAIN from wave 8 onwards, which we developed using the data in waves 1–7 using the variables EDNEW, JSTAT, JBED and NEMST.

## Independent variables

*Time*. As a category variable where each year (or data collection wave) represented a value.

*Gender*. As a dichotomous variable where male = 1 and female = 0.

*Age*. As a category variable where the continuous variable age in years identified by year of birth was recoded as follows: 16–24 = 1, 25–34 = 2, 35–44 = 3, 45–54 = 4, 55–64 = 5, 65+ = 6.

*Social class*. As a category variable that involved recoding individual's responses to the 'jbsec' item to create two social class variables. One used the Registrar General's Social Classes six value labels where 1 = professional etc. occupations (A), 2 = managerial and technical occupations (B), 3 = skilled occupations (non-manual) (C1), 4 = skilled occupations (manual) (C2), 5 = partly skilled occupations (D), and 6 = unskilled occupations (E). This variable allowed us to draw direct comparisons with recent national surveys. Our second variable used the new Socio-economic Classification values labels 1–5 where 1 = class 1, etc. We used this more inclusive social class variable for within BHPS comparisons. In both cases category allocation was done using dummy variables for each category where yes = 1 and no = 0.

*Disabled.* (objective measure): As a dichotomous variable where in receipt of Disability Living Allowance (DLA) = 1 and not in receipt of DLA = 0.

*Disabled.* (subjective measure): As a dichotomous variable using the question, 'does your heath prohibit some types of work' where yes = 1 and no = 0.

*Country of UK.* As a category variable for country of residence where the item 'region' 1–16 = England, Wales = 17, Scotland = 18, Northern Ireland = 19.

*Place of part-time training or education.* As a category variable in answer to the question, 'Where was the main place that this course or training took place?' where we grouped and coded the response options as follows: current workplace + former workplace + employer's training centre = employer = 5; private training centre = private = 4; job centre + job club = job centre/club = 3; Higher or Further Education college + adult education centre + university = education institution = 2; at or from own home + other = home/other = 1. Only individuals who answered 'yes' to our dependent variable were routed to answer this question.

*Household tenure status.* A derived dichotomous variable indexing the ownership tenure of their living accommodation at the time of the interview. 'Owner occupier' was defined as owning their home outright or owning it with a mortgage. 'Not owner occupier' was derived from a range of rented categories: local authority rented; Household Association rented; rented from employer; rented privately (furnished or unfurnished); and 'other rented'.

*Employment status.* As a category variable, being (or not being) in the workforce at the time of the interview irrespective of whether they were self-employed or employed on a part- or full-time basis. This meant we tapped into those who were out of the workforce not just for reasons of unemployment, but also because of illness, disability, caring for dependents, or other such reasons.

*Marital status.* As a category variable defined by its legal status meaning that the single, divorced and those who were in a state of co-habitation or civil partnership at the time of the interview were classified as 'not married'.

*Parenthood status.* As a category variable defined in terms of whether each respondent had dependent children living with them, irrespective of whether they were the birth parent or not. This variable thus included women who were responsible for their natural children, adopted children or stepchildren at the time of the interview. Our data did not allow us to differentiate. Dependent children were identified as those under the age of sixteen.

*Qualifications.* As a category variable where specific qualifications varied across time in accordance with current policy.

*Income status.* As a category variable according to household income, broken into quartiles, e.g. a household an individual belonged to was designated as 'poor' if it fell into the bottom quartile of household incomes for that wave.

Other variables used were: age when respondent left school; year respondent first left full-time education; type of school attended (as a category variable: comprehensive, grammar not fee paying, grammar fee paying, sixth form college, public and other private, elementary, secondary modern, technical, other); highest qualification in 1992; housing tenure in 1992 (as a category variable: owned outright, owned with mortgage, local authority rented, housing association rented, rented from employer, rented private unfurnished, rented private furnished, other rented); father's occupational social class at age fourteen (as a registrar category variable: professional, managerial and technical, skilled non-manual, skilled manual, partly skilled, unskilled occupation; not working); mother's occupational social class at age fourteen (as father's); father's educational qualifications (as a category variable: never went to school, left school no qualifications, left school with some qualifications, got further education qualifications, got university/higher qualifications); mother's educational qualifications (as father's). For these latter variables, natural father and mother or step-parents were used but where a respondent was without a father at age fourteen, mother's occupational social class only was used and vice versa if a respondent was without mother.

## Design of derived samples and statistical modelling of predictors

### Patterns and trends in participation (1998–2003)

Our samples only include those respondents who were in full-time education at school, college or university if, during the same time frame of a given wave, they had also attended part-time education or training. For analyses comparing data from Scotland and Wales, as opposed to UK level analyses, we used only data drawn from waves 9–13, which included the more geographically representative populations resulting from the addition of the 1999 Scottish and Welsh extension samples. Northern Ireland only entered the BHPS in 2001 for the first time. Hence comparative samples for all four home nations were only available from 2001. As attrition in terms of loss of membership, the effects of item non-response and accounting for population changes, for our sample is known, BHPS constructed compensatory weights were used.

### The timing and occurrence of first participation event amongst 1997 leavers

Our analytic tool for studying the time between the two events, leaving full-time initial education and returning to adult education for the first time, was discrete event history modelling. We measured this interval by tracking a cohort of initial phase leavers over a seven-year period. Our longitudinal data source was the BHPS waves 8 to 14 (1998–2004). All those in the data set who left initial phase full-time education in 1997 in England and who had been interviewed at each data collection wave for seven years (1997–2004) were eligible to enter our sample ($n = 422$). Thus, in the year prior to the 1998 data collection wave, all our sample members had experienced event 1 (leaving full-time initial education) but had yet to experience event 2 (returning to adult education). Our target event (event 2) was the first occasion that this cohort of individuals experienced adult education. We operationalised this event in terms of whether our sample answered 'yes' or 'no' to the TRAIN variable, as above.

Our metric for recording the passage of time between event 1 and event 2 was the survey's annual data collection waves. Our interest was in assessing the probability of each sample member experiencing the target event in discrete twelve-month intervals. If an individual 'survived' the first discrete time frame without having experienced the event they moved to the next time frame, and so on. As soon as they experienced the target event they dropped out of the analysis. Inevitably this meant there would be cases that would leave at the end of the observation period without having experienced the event. These were the individuals for whom information on the occurrence and timing of the target is not available. And, because these cases have to be, by definition, excluded from the analysis, the application of regular statistical tools such as means and standard deviations is inappropriate. To get round this problem the main tool for describing event occurrence is the 'life table', which provides three key statistical ways of summarizing data: the median lifetime, the hazard function and the survival function. The median lifetime identifies the point in time at which half the sample members are estimated to have experienced the target event. The hazard function assesses the risk of the target event occurring among those eligible to experience it within each discrete time period. The survivor function assessed the probability that a given individual will survive from one discrete period to the next without having experienced the event.

We first calculated the hazard functions, survivor functions and median lifetimes for each of our predictors and found them to be different for each dichotomous subgroup. Informed by these exploratory analyses we specified a discrete-time hazard model to evaluate the effects of all our predictors upon the likelihood of first participation among our sample (maximum likelihood estimation, deviance based hypothesis tests).

For each model the beta coefficient (logit), its standard error, and the odds ratio was computed. Using the log-likelihood statistic we computed a deviance statistic (–2*log likelihood) and compared deviance statistics for models that differed only by a single substantive predictor. This allowed us to evaluate the statistical significance of that predictor. Using this approach, we were able to carry out deviance-based hypothesis tests for our individual predictors and evaluate their effects. We allowed each model, including our baseline model, to include the time indicator TSQ. TSQ has a particular purpose in this analysis. We reasoned that, rather than present results with a parameter estimate of the hazard function and asymptotic standard errors for each wave over time and include dummy variables for each year as well as our covariates, we could approximate the hazard over time by including a new variable, TSQ. TSQ thus is a quadratic function of time measured by waves. Using an uncontrolled deviance-based hypothesis test we were able to evaluate the statistical significance of a single predictor.

*Mapping trajectories of participation across the life span*

We adopted a two-stage latent class model approach to identify configurations of social roles over time and life paths that link these role configurations over time. This methodological approach views individuals as being probabilistically distributed across various role configurations and life paths. It assumes underlying categories by seeking out sub-groups or collectives within populations. Like all classification systems, it involves a process of dividing a large heterogeneous group into smaller homogeneous groups where members are similar to each other while different from individuals in other groups. We use classifications as a means of tracking individual lifecourse pathways. A major advantage of applying the latent class modelling approach to our data was that it permitted the use of categorical variables without any estimation threats. The longitudinal structure of the BHPS allowed us to model the lifecourse over an extended

*Table A.1* Three BHPS cohorts of original sample members

| 1991 | Age 20–25 (n = 540) b. 1966–1971 | 40–45 (n = 604) b. 1946–1951 | 61–66 (n = 346) b. 1925–1930 |
|---|---|---|---|
| 1992 1993 1994 1995 | 24–29 | 44–49 | 65–70 |
| 1996 1997 1998 1999 2000 | 29–34 | 49–54 | 70–75 |
| 2001 2002 2003 2004 2005 | 34–39 | 54–59 | 75–80 |

period of time. Our analytic samples in this analysis consisted of three cohorts of original sample members (see Table A.1).

For each cohort sample we used six adjacent birth cohorts (e.g. b. 1966–1971) to increase our sample size and statistical power. This enhanced our ability to consider greater homogeneity in the structure of the lifecourse. At the same time these cohorts were closely related in historical time and were thus likely to have experienced unique cohort or period effects that could also have impacted upon the structure of the lifecourse.

We began our analysis by examining the appropriateness of fit of statistical models for each social role entered into the model. We examined their joint occurrence at four time points, 1991, 1995, 2000 and 2005. Our choice of time points was made on theoretical and empirical grounds. Since our interest was to broadly map the lifecourse over an extended period of time, we took the first and last points of data collection available to us (1991 and 2005 covering a 15-year period) and two points roughly evenly spaced in between. We calculated the chi-square statistic ($\chi^2$) of each model, its significance emphasizing local independence, the likelihood chi-square statistic ($L^2$), degrees of freedom ($df$), the index of dissimilarity (D), Raftery's (1995) Bayesian Information Criterion (BIC) and Akaike's (1974) Information Criterion (AIC). These were a null (one-class) model, a two-class model, a three-class model and a four-class model. The models indicated the number of classes of latent role configurations that effectively characterised the sample at each age. As the models were not hierarchical, model selection was based on overall appropriateness of fit.

## Dynamics of adult participation in part-time education and training

The data used for this analysis came from waves 2–15 (1992–2005), using the single item TRAIN from 1998 onwards to cover all respondents and the derived variable (see above) for waves 2–7. We did not use wave 1 for this analysis as EDNEW and JBED were both routed questions at this wave and, as we wished to follow a balanced sample over time, we excluded wave 1 from the analysis since these items did not cover all panel members. Our subsample of 4,325 individuals drawn from within the broader BHPS sample was picked up in 1992 and followed through to 2005. This meant that our sample was made up of respondents who had provided the relevant information on our dependent variable at all fourteen waves and who had also not participated in full-time education at any point during the full fourteen-year observation period.

To keep our sample representative of the UK population over time we used the recommended longitudinal weights. These took account of attrition in terms of loss of membership and the effects of item and wave non-response as well for population changes. All panel members had to be over sixteen years old. The age and gender profile of our sample in 1992 was as follows: 16–34 ($n$ = 1374, $f$ = 753, $m$ = 621), 35–54 ($n$ = 1856, $f$ = 1002, $m$ = 854), 55–64 ($n$ = 617, $f$ = 338, $m$ = 279) and 65+ ($n$ = 478, $f$= 294, $m$ = 184). We calculated the stocks and net flows between states and used latent class models to characterise those who were deemed to be non-participants, infrequent participants and frequent participants when followed over time.

*Qualifications trajectories (1992–2005)*

This analysis tracked the subsample of individuals ($n$ = 4,325) in the section above and monitored outcomes of each participation spell undertaken between 1992 and 2005 in terms of qualifications attained. The standard of highest existing and each new qualification was classified in terms of the UK level of qualifications framework. The BHPS contains two derived variables for highest educational qualifications attained, *highest academic or vocational qualifications* and *highest academic qualifications*. These variables are updated each year to include the most recent qualifications of panel members. We operationalised different levels of qualifications by devising a simple classification measure so that we could distinguish between different types and levels of qualifications. We then compared each new qualification attained with existing highest qualification using the national qualifications framework. In this way we followed the same individuals across time to discern if a new qualification was at a higher, similar or lower level than their highest previously achieved qualification.

# Bibliography

Akaike, H. (1974) 'A new look at the statistical model identification', *IEEE Transactions on Automatic Control* 19, 716–723.

Aldridge, F. and Tuckett, A. (2007) *The Road to Nowhere? the NIACE survey on adult participation in learning 2007*, Leicester: NIACE.

Alheit, P. (1994) *Taking the Knocks: youth unemployment and biography*, London: Cassell.

Alheit, P. (2003) 'Mentalität und Intergenerationalität als Rahmenbedingungen "Lebenslangen Lernens". Konzeptionelle Konsequenzen aus Ergebnissen einer biographieanalytischen Mehrgenerationenstudie in Ostdeutschland', *Zeitschrift für Pädagogik* 49, 362–382.

Alanen, L. (2001) 'Explorations in generational analysis', in L. Alanen and B. Mayall (eds), *Conceptualising Child–Adult Relations,* London: RoutledgeFalmer.

Antikainen, A., Houtsonen, J., Huotelin, H. and Kauppila, J. (1996) *Living in a Learning Society: life-histories,identities and education*, London: Falmer

Aro, M., Rinne, R., Lahti, K. and Olkinuora, E. (2005) 'Education or learning on the job? Generational differences of opinions in Finland', *International Journal of Lifelong Education* 24, 459–474.

Ball, S. J., Maguire, M. and Macrae, S. (2000) *Choice, Pathways and Transitions Post-16: new youth, new economies in the global city*, London: RoutledgeFalmer.

Barton, D., Ivanič, R., Appleby, Y., Hodge, R. and Tusting, K. (2007) *Literacy, Lives and Learning*, London: Routledge.

Beck, K. (2003) *Evaluation and Assessment of Flexibility, Mobility and Transferability in European Countries*, Luxembourg: Office for Official Publications of the European Communities.

Biesta, G. J. J. (2004) 'Against learning: reclaiming a language for education in an age of learning', *Nordisk Pedagogik* 23, 70–82.

Biesta, G. J. J. (2006) 'What's the point of lifelong learning if lifelong learning has no point? On the democratic deficit of policies for lifelong learning. *European Educational Research Journal* 5(3–4), 169–180.

Biesta, G. J. J. and Burbules, N. (2003) *Pragmatism and Educational Research*. Lanham, MD: Rowman & Littlefield.

Biesta, G. J. J, and Tedder, M. (2007) 'Agency and learning in the lifecourse: towards an ecological perspective', *Studies in the Education of Adults* 39, 132–149.

Bloomer, M. and Hodkinson, P. (2000) 'Learning careers: continuity and change in young people's dispositions to learning', *British Educational Research Journal* 26, 583–597.

Blundell, R., Dearden, L., Goodman, A. and Reed, H. (2000) 'The returns to higher education in Britain: evidence from a British cohort', *Economic Journal* 111, 82–99.

Boshier, R. (1998) 'Edgar Faure after 25 years: down but not out', in J. Holford, P. Jarvis and C. Griffin (eds) *International Perspectives on Lifelong Learning*, London: Kogan Page.

Boström, A. K. (2003) 'Lifelong learning, intergenerational learning and social capital: from theory to practice', PhD Thesis, University of Stockholm.

Bourdieu, P. (1984) *Distinction: a social critique of the judgement of taste*, London: Routledge.

Bourdieu, P and Wacquant, L. (1992) *An Invitation to Reflexive Sociology*, Cambridge: Polity.

Brown, J. S., Collins, A., and Duguid, P. (1989) 'Situated cognition and the culture of learning', *Educational Researcher* 18, 32–42.

Bruner, J. (1990) *Acts of Meaning,* Cambridge, MA and London: Harvard University Press.

Bude, H. (2000) 'Die biographische Relevanz der Generation', in M. Kohli and M. Szydlik (eds) *Generationen in Familie und Gesellschaft*, Opladen: Leske & Budrich.

Burke, K. (1945) *A Grammar of Motives,* Berkeley, CA: University of California Press.

CEDEFOP (2009) *European Guidelines for Validating Non-formal and Informal Learning.* Luxembourg: Centre pour la développement de la formation professionelle.

Cobb, P. and Bowers, J. (1999) 'Cognitive and situated learning perspectives in theory and practice', *Educational Researcher* 28, 4–15.

Cochinaux, P. and de Woot, P. (1995) *Moving Towards a Learning Society*, Brussels/Paris: Conseil des Recteurs Européens/European Roundtable of Employers.

Colley, H., Hodkinson, P. and Malcolm, J. (2003) *Informality and Formality in Learning: a report for the Learning and Skills Research Centre,* London: Learning and Skills Research Centre.

Crossan, B., Field, J., Gallacher, J. and Merrill, B. (2003) 'Understanding participation in learning for non-traditional adult learners: learning careers and the construction of learning identities', *British Journal of Sociology of Education* 24, 55–67.

Czarniawska, B. (2004) *Narratives in Social Science Research,* London: Sage

Daniels, H. (2001) *Vygotsky and Pedagogy*. London: RoutledgeFalmer.

Dausien, B. (1998) 'Biographische Konstruktionen in Widersprüchen', in K. Weber (ed.) *Life History, Gender and Experience: theoretical approaches to adult life and learning*, Roskilde: Adult Education Research Group, Roskilde University.

Denham, J. (2007) 'New higher education funding incentives, 2008–11', London: Department of Innovation, Universities and Skills, www.hefce.ac.uk/news/hefce/2007/HEFCE_letterELQ.pdf (accessed 25 July 2010).

Dominicé, P. (2000) *Learning From Our Lives: using educational biographies with adults*, San Francisco, CA: Jossey-Bass.

Eccarius, J. (2002) 'Generation und Bildung. Eine historische und systematische Betrachtung unter besonderer Berücksichtigung des Bildungsbegriffs und der schulischen Bildung', in R. Tippelt (ed.) *Handbuch Bildungsforschung*, Opladen: Leske and Budrich.

Emirbayer, M. and Mische, A. (1998) 'What is agency?' *American Journal of Sociology* 103, 962–1023.

Engeström, Y. (1999) 'Activity theory and individual and social transformation', in Y. Engeström, R. Miettinen, and R. Punamaki (eds) *Perspectives on Activity Theory*. Cambridge: Cambridge University Press.

Faure, E., Herrera, P., Kaddoura, A., Lopes, H., Petrovsky, A. V., Rahnema, A. and Ward, F. C. (1972) *Learning to Be: the world of education today and tomorrow*, Paris: UNESCO.

Felstead, A., Fuller, A., Jewson, N. and Unwin, L. (2009) *Improving Working as Learning*, London: Routledge.

Field, J. (2006) *Lifelong Learning and the New Educational Order*, 2nd edn, Stoke-on-Trent: Trentham.

Field, J. (2007) 'Behaviourism and training: the programmed instruction movement in Britain', *Journal of Vocational Education and Training* 59, 313–329.

Field, J. (with H. Lynch and I. Malcolm) (2008) 'Generations, the life course and lifelong learning'. Summative working paper 3, Exeter/Stirling: The Learning Lives Project, available at www.learninglives.org.

Field, J. and Spence, L. (2000) 'Informal learning and social capital', in F. Coffield (ed.) *The Necessity of Informal Learning*, Bristol: Policy Press.

Gardner, J. (ed.) (2006) *Assessment and Learning*, London: Sage.

Giddens, A. (1991) *Modernity and Self-identity: self and society in the late modern age*, Cambridge: Polity.

Goodson, I. F. (2006) 'The rise of the life narrative', *Teacher Education Quarterly* 33, 7–21.

Goodson, I. and Sikes, P. (2001) *Life History Research in Educational Settings: learning from lives*, Buckingham: Open University Press.

Goodson, I., Biesta, G.J.J., Tedder, M. and Adair, N. (2010) *Narrative Learning*, London/New York: Routledge.

Gorard, S., Rees, G. and Fevre, R. (1999) 'Patterns of participation in lifelong learning: do families make a difference?', *British Educational Research Journal*, 25, 517-532.

Gorard, S. and Rees, G. (2002) *Creating a Learning Society? Learning careers and policies for lifelong learning*, Bristol: Policy Press.

Grace, A. P. (2004) 'Lifelong learning as a chameleonic concept and versatile practice: Y2K perspectives and trends', *International Journal of Lifelong Education* 23, 385–405.

Hager, P. (2005) 'Current theories of workplace learning: a critical assessment', in N. Bascia, A. Cumming, K. Datnow, K. Leitwood and D. Livingstone (eds) *International Handbook of Educational Policy*, Dordrecht: Springer.

Hammarström, G. (2004) 'The constructs of generation and cohort in sociological studies of aging: theoretical conceptualisation and some empirical implications', in B.-M. Öberg, A.L. Närvänen, E. Näsman and E. Olssen (eds) *Changing Worlds and the Changing Subject: dimensions in the study of later life*, Aldershot: Ashgate.

Heath, S., Fuller, A. and Paton, K. (2007) 'Life course, generation, and educational decision-making within networks of intimacy', paper presented at British Educational Research Association Annual Conference, London.

Hodkinson, P. (2005) 'Learning as cultural and relational: moving past some troubling dualisms', *Cambridge Journal of Education* 35, 107–119.

Hodkinson, P., Sparkes, A. and Hodkinson, H. (1996) *Triumphs and Tears: young people, markets and the transition from school to work*, London: David Fulton.

Hodkinson, P., Biesta, G.J.J., Gleeson, D., James, D. and Postlethwaite, K.C. (2005) 'The heuristic and holistic synthesis of large volumes of qualitative data', paper presented at the Research Capacity Building Network Annual Conference, Cardiff.

Hodkinson, P., Biesta, G. and James, D. (2007) 'Understanding learning cultures', *Educational Review* 59, 415–427.

Hodkinson, P., Biesta, G. and James, D. (2008a) 'Understanding learning culturally: overcoming the dualism between social and individual views of learning', *Vocations and Learning* 1, 27–47.

Hodkinson, P., Ford, G., Hodkinson, H. and Hawthorne, R. (2008b) 'Retirement as a learning process', *Educational Gerontology* 34, 167–184.

Houten, C. van (1998) *Erwachsenenbildung als Schicksalspraxis: Grundlagen für zeitgemässes Lernen*, Stuttgart: Verlag Freies Geistesleben.

Hyde, M., Wiggins, R.D., Higgs, P. and Blane, D.B. (2003) 'A measure of quality of life in early old age: the theory, development and properties of a needs satisfaction model (CASP-19)', *Aging & Mental Health* 7, 186–194.

Institute for Social and Economic Research (2010) British Household Panel Survey, www.iser.essex.ac.uk/survey/bhps (accessed 27 July 2010).

Istance, D. (2003) 'Schooling and lifelong learning: insights from OECD analyses', *European Journal of Education* 38, 85–98.

James, D. and Biesta, G.J.J. (2007). *Improving Learning Cultures in Further Education*, London: Routledge.

Kohli, M. (2003) *Generationen in der Gesellschaft*, Forschungsbericht 73. Berlin: Forschungsgruppe Altern und Lebenslauf.

Kenner, C., Mahera, R., Jessel, J., Gregory, E. and Arju, T. (2007) 'Intergenerational learning between children and grandparents in East London', *Journal of Early Childhood Research* 5, 219–243.

Lang, I. and Canning, R. (2010) 'The use of citations in educational research: the instance of the concept of "situated learning"', *Journal of Further and Higher Education* 34, 291–301.

Lave, J. and Wenger, E. (1991) *Situated Learning: legitimate peripheral participation*, Cambridge. Cambridge University Press.

Macleod, F. and Lambe, P. (2007) 'Patterns and trends in part-time adult education participation in relation to UK nation, class, place of participation, gender, age and disability, 1998–2003', *International Journal of Lifelong Education* 26, 399–418.

Macleod, F. and Lambe, P. (2008) 'Dynamics of adult participation in part-time education and training: results from the British Household Panel Survey', *Research Papers in Education* 23, 231–241.

Mannheim, K. (1952) *Ideology and Utopia: an introduction to the sociology of knowledge*, London: Routledge.

Martin, I. (2002) 'Adult education, lifelong learning and citizenship: some ifs and buts', *International Journal of Lifelong Education*, 22, 566–579.

McGivney, V. (2006) 'Attracting new groups into learning: lessons from research in England', in J. Chapman, P. Cartwright and E. McGilp (eds), *Lifelong Learning, Participation and Equity*, Dordrecht: Springer.

McMullin, J. A., Comeau, T. D. and Jovic, E. (2007) 'Generational affinities and discourses of difference: a case study of highly skilled information technology workers', *British Journal of Sociology* 58, 297–316.

Nielsen, H. B. and Rudberg, M. (2000) 'Gender, love and education in three generations: the way out and up', *European Journal of Women's Studies* 17, 423–453.

OECD (1997) *Lifelong Learning for All*, Paris: Organisation for Economic Co-operation and Development.

Olkinuora, E., Rinne, R., Mäkinen, J., Järvinen, T. and Jauhaiainen, A. (2008) 'Promises and risks of the learning society: the meanings of lifelong learning for three Finnish generations', *Studies in the Education of Adults* 40, 40–61

Paterson, L. and Iannelli, C. (2007) 'Social class and educational attainment: a comparative study of England, Wales and Scotland', *Sociology of Education* 80, 330–358.

Phillips, T. and Western, M. (2005) 'Social change and social identity: post-modernity, reflexive modernisation and the transformation of social identities in Australia', in F. Devine, M. Savage, J. Scott and R. Crompton (eds) *Rethinking Class: culture, identities and lifestyle*, Basingstoke: Palgrave Macmillan.

Piaget, J. (1952) *The Origins of Intelligence in Children*, New York: International Press.

Polkinghorne, D. (1988) *Narrative Knowing and the Human Sciences*. Albany, NY: SUNY Press.

Polkinghorne, D. (1995) 'Narrative configuration in qualitative analysis', in J.A. Hatch and R. Wisniewski (eds) *Life History and Narrative,* London: Falmer

Raffe, D. (2008) 'As others see us: a commentary on the OECD review of the quality and equity of schooling in Scotland', *Scottish Educational Review* 40, 22–36.

Raftery, A. E. (1995) 'Bayesian model selection in social research', *Sociological Methodology* 25, 111–196.

Ranson, S., Martin, J., Nixon, J. and P. McKeown (1996) 'Towards a theory of learning', *British Journal of Educational Studies* 44, 9–26.

Ricoeur, P. (1991) 'Life in quest of narrative', in D. Wood (ed.) *On Paul Ricoeur: narrative and interpretation,* London: Routledge.

Rogers, C. (1969) *Freedom to Learn: a view of what education might become,* Columbus, OH: Merill.

Rogoff, B. (2003) *The Cultural Nature of Human Development,* Oxford: Oxford University Press.

Rossiter, M. and Clark, M.C. (2007) *Narrative and the Practice of Adult Education,* Malabar, FL: Krieger.

Sfard, A. (1998) 'On two metaphors of learning and the dangers of choosing just one', *Educational Researcher* 27, 4–13.

Springate, I., Atkinson, M. and Martin, K. (2008) *Intergenerational Practice: a review of the literature,* Slough: National Foundation for Educational Research.

Straka, G. A. (2004) *Informal Learning: genealogy, concept, antagonisms and questions,* Bremen: Institut Technik und Bildung.

Strauss, A. (1962) 'Transformations of identity', in A. Rose (ed.) *Human Behavior and Social Processes,* Boston, MA: Houghton-Mifflin.

Tedder, M. and Biesta, G.J.J. (2009a) 'Biography, transition and learning in the lifecourse: the role of narrative', in J. Field, J. Gallacher and R. Ingram (eds) *Resarching Transitions in Lifelong Learning,* London: Routledge.

Tedder, M. and Biesta, G.J.J. (2009b) 'What does it take to learn from one's life? Exploring opportunities for biographical learning in the lifecourse', in B. Merrill (ed.) *Learning to Change? The role of identity and learning careers in adult education,* Frankfurt am Main: Peter Lang.

Tennant, M. (1997) *Psychology and Adult Learning,* London: Routledge

Tuckett, A. and Aldridge, F. (2010) *A Change for the Better: the NIACE survey on adult participation in learning 2010,* Leicester: NIACE.

Wenger, E. (1998) *Communities of Practice: learning, meaning and identity,* Cambridge: Cambridge University Press.

Wertsch, J. W. (1998) *Mind as Action,* Oxford: Oxford University Press

West, L. (1996) *Beyond Fragments: adults, motivation and higher education – a biographical analysis,* London: Taylor & Francis.

# Index